MAPS IN CONTEXT
A Workbook for American History
Volume 2: From 1865

Gerald A. Danzer
University of Illinois at Chicago

Bedford/St. Martin's
Boston   ◆   New York

Contents

Introduction

Maps and historical studies have much in common: both use art and science to create representations of things we cannot experience directly. In the case of maps, most spaces are too vast and the geography too complex to be understood with a single look. History has an additional challenge: the past has forever slipped away and we need devices to help us recover and understand it. Both the cartographer (or map maker) and the historian start by gathering facts, but they are quickly overwhelmed with data, presenting the need to select, shorten, and clarify their portrayals. The cartographer turns to symbols and visual images while the historian depends primarily on words and concepts. Working together, the historian and the cartographer combine their talents to craft a coherent narrative about the past.

Our conviction is that encouraging students to think geographically will help them to think historically. And *visa versa*. The ultimate goal of geography and history is the same—both attempt to make connections to larger pictures, to see places and events as part of a greater whole. Although geography and history have separate and distinct modes of explanation, ways of asking questions, and styles of appreciation, they rely on each other to present the most complete story possible.

Thus, to excel as a student of American history, some geography is necessary. This workbook for beginners aims to get you started and to offer encouragement along the way. It uses maps as a natural arena where geography and history come together. Each lesson features an historical map, a selected image of the earth drawn today to help us imagine what the world looked like in the past. As models of reality, historical maps extract certain features for emphasis to make the world intelligible. Above all, historical maps are instructional devices, and the cartographer always follows a lesson plan. One way to begin reading a map is to figure out the purpose of the lesson. Stated another way, there is a teacher behind every map.

While historical maps aim to simplify, they are not simple devices. They are quite complicated in their own way and often remind us of the complexity of the human experience as they try to reduce past events to an orderly picture. Just as students of geography, students of history must be cartographically literate—that is, have the ability to read and understand maps of all types. The plan of this workbook is to provide a series of maps accompanied by worksheets to guide students through American history by developing a geographic context. In the process, cartographic literacy will come naturally and, we trust, so will geographical and historical patterns of thought.

This workbook is organized in three sections. Section one, "Basic Geography," works to establish the geographic context of American history and introduces the core themes of geography – location, place, region, movement, and interaction. Section two, "Mapping America's History," explores in a chronological manner a variety of topics, events, movements, and concepts that are essential parts of the basic structure of any American history course. Section three, "One-Minute Map Quizzes" provides a series of brief quizzes to help you check your knowledge of key places in America's story. The Appendix includes an answer key, and also several American and World outline reference maps.

Every "Basic Geography" and "Mapping America's History" worksheet has three parts. First, "Maptalk" presents a general discussion about the map in its historical context. These introductions are designed to provide a way of thinking about the map in its active teaching role. Second, "Reading the Map" highlights several specific things to look for on the map that will help it become a useful learning device. Third, "Working with the Map," suggests one or more short activities designed to pull it all together. Many of these activities are open-ended with no "correct answers", allowing instructors maximum flexibility to adapt the workbook material to their own teaching style.

More than a collection of exercises focused on a particular area of study, a workbook is connected to an approach to education based on active learning. As a companion to your American history textbook, *Maps in Context* provides a rich collection of hands-on lessons to help you develop your skills in thinking both geographically and historically—and to understand the essential connections between the two. Both are avenues to human understanding and self-awareness. We wish you every success on your journey.

Gerald A. Danzer
University of Illinois at Chicago

Basic Geography

The World on a Mercator Projection

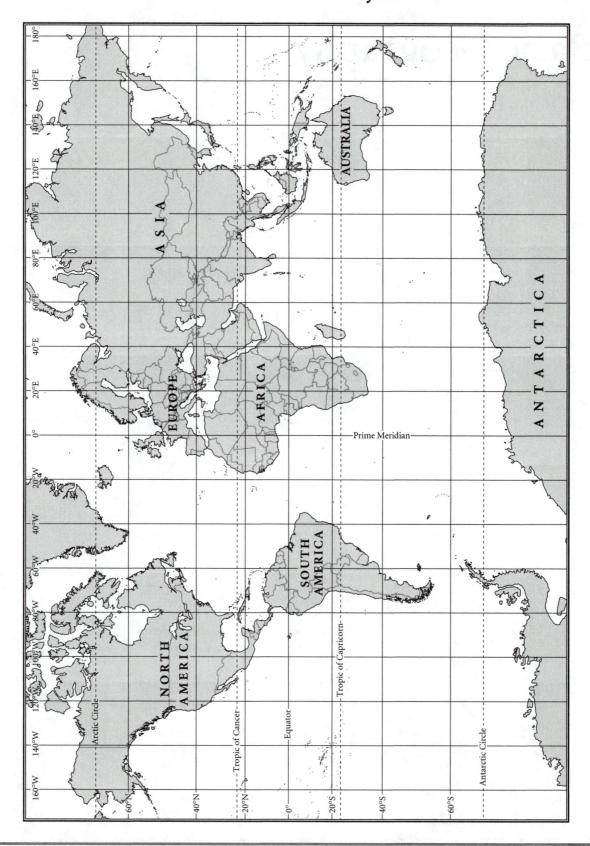

Maptalk: Location

In many ways, all history courses start with a world map. In studying the past to gain some insight into the human condition, a global stage is needed because over thousands of generations humanity has migrated over the earth. This story of migration is especially applicable to American history as it is studied and taught today: a meeting place where various peoples have come together to fashion a new society and culture.

Maps are the best devices to show location, and any place on a map is located in reference to the earth as a whole. Of the many ways in which the earth can be mapped as a complete unit, the Mercator projection is probably the most familiar. A map projection is any technique used to transfer an image of the three-dimensional earth to a two-dimensional sheet of paper. Every approach tries to preserve some feature of the earth's surface, like area, direction, or distance, and in the process distorts others. In 1569 the Flemish cartographer Gerardus Mercator, by trial and error, worked out a formula so that any great circle on the globe would be a straight line on a map. Mercator stretched the map in a way that results in great distortions in distance and area as one proceeds poleward, but preserves true direction. This was a notable achievement in a seafaring society dependent on accurate information for navigation.

The rectangular grid of Mercator's map makes it easy to find locations using a global position of "latitude" and "longitude." Lines of latitude circle the globe east to west and are called *parallels*. Lines of longitude circle the globe north to south and are called *meridians*. This system of lines is sometimes called absolute location. Relative location, thinking about a place in terms of its surroundings rather than its precise site, is also encouraged by the Mercator projection because the directions are always true, running as straight lines on the map. Thus it is easy to see that South America lies considerably east of North America.

Reading the Map

1. Note that the sizes of areas pictured at the top and bottom of the map are quite distorted. Greenland, which looks like a continent on the map, is really less than one-third the size of Australia and less than one-eight the size of South America.

2. The equator spans all the points on the earth's surface that are midway between the poles. Near the equator the sun shines with its greatest strength, making the equatorial regions the hottest climates.

3. The Tropic of Cancer in the Northern Hemisphere and the Tropic of Capricorn in the Southern Hemisphere mark the end of the tropical regions, places where the sun shines directly overhead during the entire year.

4. The Arctic Circle and the Antarctic Circle, in contrast, mark the beginning of the high latitudes where during the winter, or low-sun season, there is at least one day in which the sun never gets above the horizon.

5. The middle latitudes are found between the polar regions and the tropics. These are regions of temperate climates, usually with distinct seasons like summer and winter, or a dry season and a wet season.

6. By international agreement, the measurement of longitude begins at the prime meridian, 0°. This meridian is a line through the observatory in Greenwich, England, a borough of London.

7. Longitude is measured both east and west of the prime meridian, reaching 180°, halfway around the world. The International Date Line runs near the 180th meridian.

Working with the Map

This exercise will help you review the basic global context for American history. Washington, D.C., has a global position of about 39° N., 77° W. Locate it on the map and extend lines in the cardinal directions (north, south, east, and west) from America's capitol. Which of the following places do these lines cross? Consult a reference atlas and mark "yes" or "no" in the spaces provided.

_____	England	_____	South Africa
_____	Spain	_____	Mexico
_____	China	_____	Canada
_____	Afghanistan	_____	Cuba
_____	Japan	_____	Russia

WORKSHEET B
The World on a Peters Equal-Area Projection

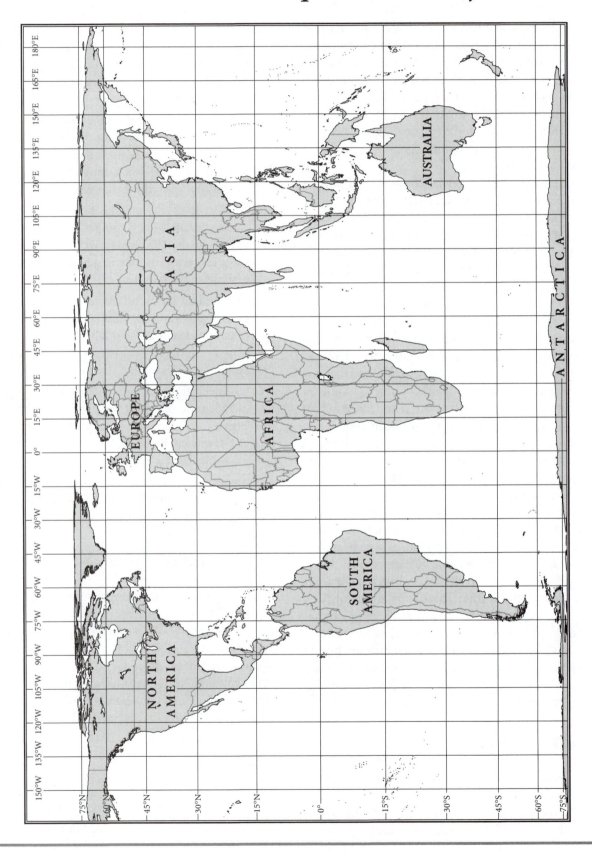

Maptalk: Location

The global position of any place expressed in terms of latitude and longitude is always the same no matter which projection is used. The Mercator projection used in Worksheet A, for example, maintains "true-direction." The one shown here is an "equal-area" presentation, first developed by James Gall in the nineteenth century. In 1973 Arno Peters, a German historian, advocated the use of this type of map to correct the area distortions of the familiar Mercator projection. Peters believed that traditional maps like Mercator's emphasized Europe and the Northern Hemisphere at the expense of the tropical region. His solution was to elongate the low latitudes and flatten the high latitudes. In the process, accuracy of direction, distance, and shape were all compromised, but the projection did show equal areas around the globe.

To correct traditional "eurocentric" maps, Peters designed his projection so that the center of the map was the point where the equator struck the Atlantic coast of Africa, about 10° east of the prime meridian (0 degrees longitude).

Reading the Map

1. The meridians on this map divide the world into twenty-four zones, one for each hour of the day. The prime meridian is set at London and the others are marked off in 15° intervals, roughly reproducing standard time zones.

2. The parallels on this map are not evenly spaced as they would be on a globe, but are adjusted for the curvature of the earth to achieve an equal-area map. Note how the parallels divide the earth into twelve zones between the poles, again set 15° apart.

3. In almost all cylindrical projections, it is very difficult to show the very high latitudes (above 80°) or to indicate the earth's poles. Note how these are flattened on this example.

4. The world's oceans are well presented on this map because it is an equal-area projection. Turning the image upside down with Antarctica at the top will emphasize the dominance of water over land on the earth's surface. Note the continuous water passage at 60° south.

Working with the Map

Because the meridians on this map are parallel it is possible to cut the image along any degree of longitude and move it to the outside edges of the map. Remove this page or make a photocopy of it. Then trim the margin on the left hand side of the map. Next cut the image along the 90th east meridian (at the Ganges Delta between India and Malaya). Move the left part of the map to the right side and tape the two parts together. North America will now be at the center of the image.

Write a caption for this new world map explaining its advantages and disadvantages for students of American history.

North American Rivers and Their Basins

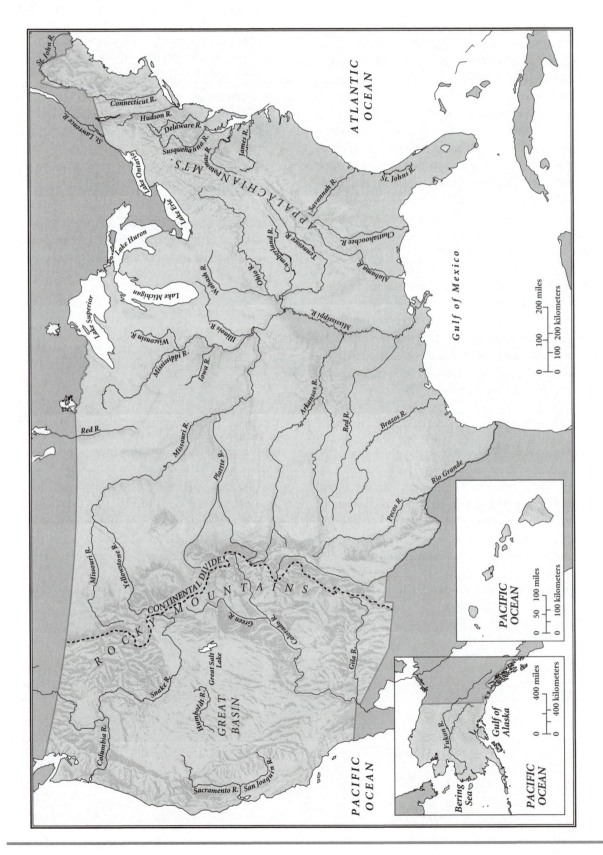

Maptalk: Place

Human activity creates places. Locations exist on their own without the presence of humans, but they become *places* when people use the spot in some way. As generation after generation uses a place, it produces artifacts, develops layers of remains, and accumulates a variety of associations held in a society's memory. At first, human activity may be passive: looking the site over, connecting it to its surroundings, noting its situation, and perhaps giving it a name. Later, humans may start to use the place in some specific way—hunting ground, campsite, field, pasture, settlement, shrine, or pathway. Through use, abstract global positions become specific places of unique character.

Places are usually on land, with readily observed physical characteristics such as topography, soils, and vegetation. Places vary in size. Some, like a field or a town, are assigned certain boundaries by humans. Others, such as rivers and their valleys or basins, are defined by nature. Some places are so circumscribed that they can be perceived at a glance, like the Great Falls of the Snake River. Others, such as the Mississippi Valley, are so vast it would take a lifetime to observe every acre of them.

Places help to give people an identity. Few people think of watersheds—rivers and their basins—when they identify with a particular place, yet rivers and their basins are important to many events in American history. Through the mid-nineteenth century in the era before railroad, highway, and air transportation made water routes less important, access to navigable rivers was crucial to exploration and migration patterns, and to the establishment of towns and cities.

Reading the Map

1. The Continental Divide separates waters flowing into the Atlantic Ocean and those heading toward the Pacific Ocean. Note how the long reach of the Missouri River pushes this line far to the west.

2. The Great Basin has no outlet to the sea. The Great Salt Lake receives much of the run-off in this region, but one river, the Humboldt, drains into a sink long before reaching the salty lake.

3. The Mississippi Valley includes the great river and all its tributaries. Waters from every state between the Appalachians and the Rockies flow toward New Orleans. \

4. Many rivers flow from the Appalachian Mountains to the Atlantic, which encouraged the formation of many states along this coast. The Pacific Slope is another story. It has only a few major rivers and only three states.

Working with the Map

On the map draw in the approximate location of the Continental Divide, the extent of the Mississippi Valley, and the reaches of the Great Basin. Use a reference map or atlas to help.

Then locate and identify on the map the following: Niagara Falls, the Grand Canyon, the Falls of St. Anthony, Yellowstone Falls, Hoover Dam, the Mississippi Delta, Lake Okeechobee.

Next locate the following cities on the map and match with their river location.

_____ 1. New York   A. Mouth of the Ohio River

_____ 2. Denver   B. Near Hoover Dam

_____ 3. Santa Fe   C. Falls of the Ohio River

_____ 4. Minneapolis D. Delaware River

_____ 5. Kansas City E. Source of the Platte

_____ 6. Louisville   F. Rio Grande

_____ 7. Philadelphia G. Mouth of the Hudson

_____ 8. Portland   H. Missouri River

_____ 9. Las Vegas   I. Mouth of the Columbia

_____10. Pittsburgh   J. Mississippi River waterfall

Geography of the United States

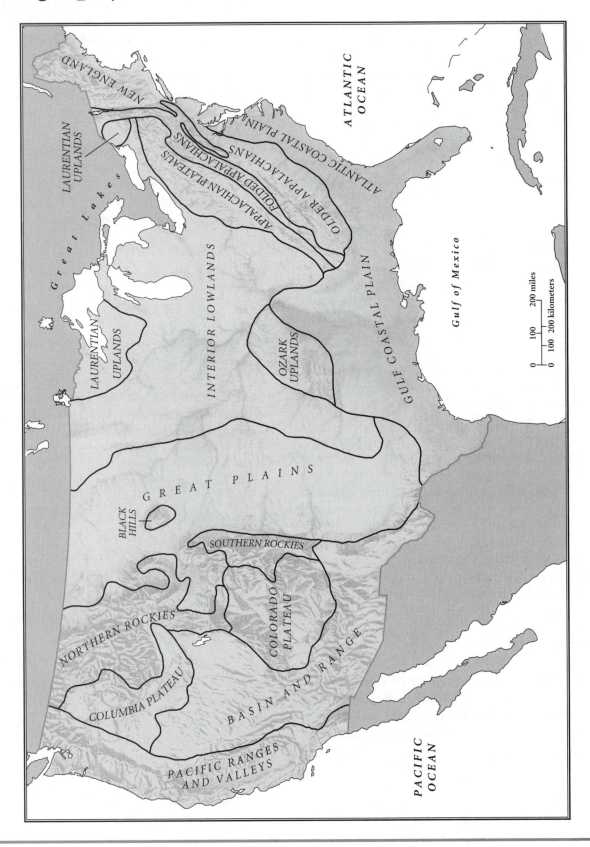

Maptalk: Region

When historians refer to the geographic setting of American history they usually mean the physical character of the land. The actual locations where events "took place" need to be imagined on any historical map. Thus, reference to an event on the Atlantic Coastal Plain, in the Rocky Mountains, or on the Colorado Plateau will spark certain pictorial images or representative landscapes in the reader's mind.

To begin the study of American history, a review of the nation's major physiographic regions is useful. A region is a group of places that share common characteristics that distinguishes them from surrounding areas. For physiographic regions, these distinguishing features are physical characteristics usually related to geological structure and its resulting topography. Thus places with a similar lay of the land, resulting from either physical features (e.g., similar rocks formation) or from the experience of a common history, are called regions.

Reading the Map

1. There are several major mountain range systems in the United States. The old Appalachian Uplands extend from Georgia and Alabama north to New York and New England.

2. The Appalachian system is a series of mountains that have been worn down over millennia by erosion. Some are folded mountains resulting from the compression of the land mass. Foothills and extensive plateaus characterize the Appalachians in the east to the Great Lakes and the Ohio Valley in the west.

3. The Midwest, south and west of the Great Lakes, is often called the Interior Lowlands.

4. The Appalachians separate the Atlantic Coastal Plain from the Interior Lowlands, a series of plains that extend across the continent. The Gulf Coastal Plain continues the Atlantic lowland west to Texas where it meets the Great Plains, a higher and drier region that reaches northward to the Arctic Ocean.

5. The mountains of the Great West start with the Rockies, a series of young ranges that rise suddenly from the Great Plains. West of the Rockies are two high plateaus named after their major rivers: the Colorado and the Columbia. Then the extensive Basin and Range area extends from west Texas to California. Most of these dry lands in Nevada and Utah lack an outlet to the sea, resulting in the Great Salt Lake and similar lakes and sinks.

6. A series of high mountain ranges, deep valleys, and lower but very rugged coastal ranges mark the Pacific coast.

Working with the Map

Consult an atlas or a reference map to locate the following places. Then place them on the map and indicate the physiographic region they are associated with.

Place	Region
_____ 1. Grand Canyon	A. Atlantic Coastal Plain
_____ 2. Detroit	B. Appalachian system
_____ 3. Spokane	C. Gulf Coastal Plain
_____ 4. Pittsburgh	D. Interior Lowlands
_____ 5. Wichita	E. Great Plains
_____ 6. Mobile	F. Rocky Mountains
_____ 7. The Chesapeake	G. Columbia Plateau
_____ 8. Death Valley	H. Colorado Plateau
_____ 9. Pike's Peak	I. Basin and Range
_____ 10. The Golden Gate	J. Pacific ranges and valleys

WORKSHEET E
The Atlantic World

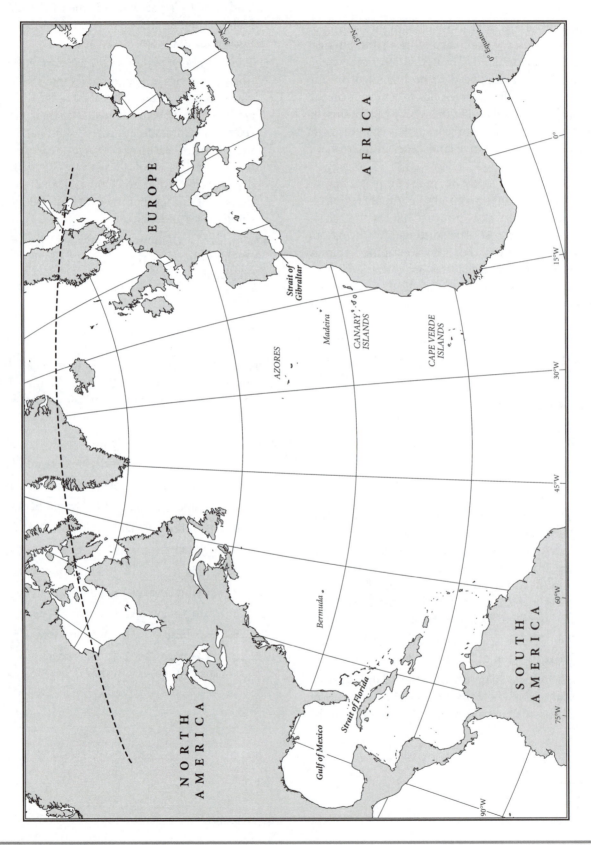

Maptalk: Movement

The concept of an Atlantic World is a key to understanding important topics in American history: the European explorations, the building of overseas empires, the African diasporas resulting from the slave trade, the great migration of peoples from Europe to the New World, the world wars of the twentieth century, and the emergence of a global economy.

The geographic theme of movement lies at the heart of the idea of an Atlantic World. Without movement back and forth across the Atlantic, we would not conceive of a region centered on an ocean. When people first began crossing the Atlantic at the end of the fifteenth century, goods, ideas, beliefs, diseases, plants, and animals traveled with them, in what is termed the "Columbian Exchange." For five centuries, the Atlantic has connected people living along its shores even as it physically separated them. The concept of an Atlantic civilization focuses on the elements connecting Europe, Africa, and the Americas.

Reading the Map

1. The projection used for this map curves both the meridians and the parallels. The result emphasizes the basin-like character of the north Atlantic Ocean.
2. Note the eastward thrust of South America. The distance from Cape Verde on the African coast to the eastern tip of South America is less than 2000 miles.
3. The Gulf of Mexico carries the waters of the Atlantic westward almost to the 98th meridian, more than one-fourth of the way around the globe. It is over 4600 miles from the Strait of Gibraltar to the Strait of Florida.
4. In the age of sail, wind patterns and currents influenced the choice of a trans-Atlantic route. In the air age, however, great circle routes such as the dotted line between central Europe and the Great Plains became the shortest routes for aircraft. Note how this pathway crosses near Iceland, Greenland, and Hudson Bay on a flight from Warsaw to Denver.
5. Europe is much further north than the Atlantic coast of the United States. Land's End at the southwestern tip of Great Britain is at 50° latitude, 11° north of Washington, D.C.

Working with the Map

To fully comprehend the patterns of European exploration and settlement in the Americas, it is helpful to understand the clockwise motion of major currents of the North Atlantic. The Canary Current starts off the Strait of Gibraltar and reaches the Cape Verde Islands before turning westward as the North Equatorial Current. This steady current is pushed by the trade winds to the West Indies. The Gulf Stream continues the circulation pattern, sending warm tropical waters through the Strait of Florida and along the Carolina coast before cutting across the ocean in a northeasterly direction, reaching from Iceland to Spain as the broad North Atlantic Drift.

Use arrows and labels to indicate the circulation patterns of currents on the map. Then consult a reference atlas and label the following places:

Sahara	Greenland
Brazil	Iceland
Panama	Great Britain
Cuba	France
Newfoundland	Spain
Caribbean Sea	Hudson Bay

Large-Scale Maps

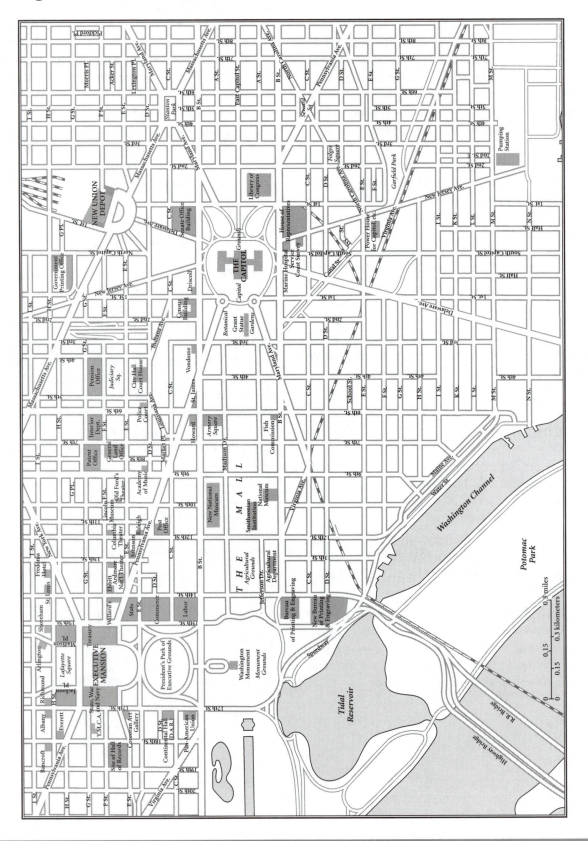

Maptalk: Interaction

A large-scale map, by definition, is one on which individual features are drawn close to the scale used for the map. On this map of Washington, D.C. in 1912, the actual outlines of the large public buildings are set to the scale of the map itself. The scale is large enough to make this possible, hence the designation as a large-scale map.

Similarly, streets and pathways, although somewhat exaggerated in size, bear a resemblance to the space they actually occupy. The importance of streets underlies magnifying their size, especially a map like this one designed to help people find their way around the city.

The large scale of this map also helps us envisage the human-environmental interaction that surrounds and influences all human activities. But on an urban street map like this, it seems like the human presence has completely taken over the natural setting and pushed nature to the margins or confined it to parks and reserves. The map reader must make the effort to keep the natural environment in mind.

Any plan for a settlement of any size shows the human pattern imposed on the land. When studied carefully, a map such as this of Washington, D.C. reveals tension between the natural topography and the geometric pattern of blocks and streets. The presence of waterways reminds readers of the natural setting because the human layout must take into account drainage patterns and tidal flows.

Reading the Map

1. Start your exploration of this map by following the shorelines that mark the boundary between land and water. The Potomac River here is part of the large estuary called Chesapeake Bay. Tidal activity is evident in the Tidal Reservoir, which holds back fresh water pushed into the reservoir with each rising tide.

2. Next, note the street pattern which separates the land into blocks and parcels set aside for public and private use. The Capitol is clearly the central focus of this urban plan because major avenues radiate from it as from the hub of a wheel. Three streets and the Mall run in the cardinal directions and divide the city into quadrants: N.W., N.E., S.W., and S.E.

3. Other major buildings include the Union Depot, which seems to rival the Capitol in size, indicating that the nation in 1912 was still in the railroad era. The Executive Mansion (White House) does not seem so imposing as a building, but the urban plan gives it status as the secondary hub. Other large buildings on the map are devoted to government functions, museum space, and headquarters for organizations.

4. Pennsylvania Avenue connects the Executive Mansion with the Capitol, with the Washington Monument serving as the third point in a large federal triangle. Note how the city planners located the obelisk slightly off center so that people at the Capitol would have an unobstructed view due west into the interior of the continent.

5. The "Mall" or park proceeding west from the Capitol to the Potomac emphasized this westward orientation for the capital city. Note how the Mall was formally subdivided in 1912 into sections used for the public gardens, Armory Square, the Smithsonian Institution, the Agricultural Grounds, and the Monument Grounds.

Working with the Map

A comparison of large-scale maps of a specific place at different time periods would demonstrate how human beings change their patterns of interaction with the landscape. Compare this map of Washington, D.C. in 1912 with a current street map of the nation's capital. Focusing on land and water use, write a paragraph detailing the major changes of the twentieth century. How might these changes be accounted for?

States: Building the Union

Maptalk: Federal and State

The federal system of United States divides the powers and responsibilities of government between the central government and the states. This division is spelled out in the federal Constitution and in the various state constitutions. Where the separation of powers is not clear, the courts, legislation, and practice all come into play. Any informed discussion of America's past recognizes the importance of elements both of cooperation and tension between states and nation that often surface in political events.

The United States emerged as a nation in the aftermath of the American Revolution—a common struggle for independence by the thirteen British North American colonies. Two types of government resulted: individual independent states and a united confederation. The Declaration referred to "these united colonies" in advancing their claim to be independent states. The development of the U.S. flag over the years recognized the thirteen original states in the stripes and *all* of the states individually in the stars.

Under the U.S. Constitution, local, state, and federal or central governments have certain powers and responsibilities. International relations are reserved to the federal government. Thus the United States is recognized by other nations as one nation and has only one vote in the United Nations. Local governments are subdivisions of the states, and the placement of local government under the jurisdiction of individual states rather than the central government has brought state government close to the everyday lives of the people.

Reading the Map

1. As the number of states grew new maps had to be created in every decade from the 1790s until 1912. At this point, all the continental territories of the U.S. had become states.

2. The District of Columbia was the only exception to the statement above. Originally part of Maryland, it was ceded to the United States for use as a capital city. Then it became a special district serving as the seat of the federal government.

3. Alaska and Hawaii, which became territories in the later nineteenth century, both became states in 1959. Note how special inset maps with individual scales are needed to include the 49th and 50th states.

4. Some residents of Puerto Rico have advocated statehood for this Caribbean island, but the majority of its people have preferred a commonwealth status instead of either statehood or independence. Puerto Rico does not appear on this map, nor does it get a star on the American flag.

Working with the Map

First test your ability to identify each of the states by placing its name or abbreviation on the map.

Next use a marker to group the states into regional clusters based on their geography and history. The U.S. Census uses nine such categories.

1. New England is made up of the six states within or east of the Connecticut River Valley.

2. The Middle Atlantic states are New York, New Jersey, and Pennsylvania.

3. The South Atlantic states include the states south of Pennsylvania all the way to Florida. West Virginia is included in this group even though it does not touch the Atlantic Ocean.

4. The East North Central states comprise those formed out of the Northwest Territory, except Minnesota.

5. The West North Central states all include territory secured in the Louisiana Purchase: Minnesota, the Dakotas, Iowa, Missouri, Kansas, and Nebraska.

6. The East South Central states are Kentucky, Tennessee, Alabama, and Mississippi, all situated south of the Ohio River.

7. The West South Central states include Texas and three states formed from the Louisiana Purchase: Louisiana, Arkansas, and Oklahoma.

8. The eight Mountain states reach from Mexico to Canada but do not touch the Pacific Ocean.

9. The Pacific states all have long coastlines along the Pacific Ocean: California, Oregon, Washington, Alaska, and Hawaii.

Mapping America's History

The Barrow Plantation, 1860 and 1881

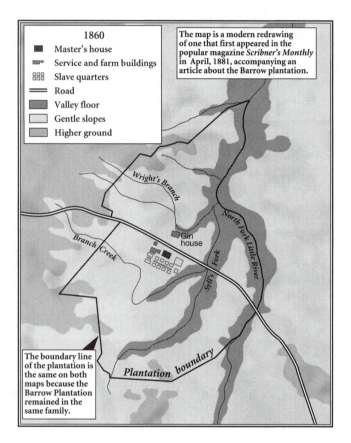

1860

- ■ Master's house
- ▭ Service and farm buildings
- ▦ Slave quarters
- ═ Road
- ▨ Valley floor
- ▢ Gentle slopes
- ▧ Higher ground

The map is a modern redrawing of one that first appeared in the popular magazine *Scribner's Monthly* in April, 1881, accompanying an article about the Barrow plantation.

Wright's Branch

Branch Creek

Gin house

Syll's Fork

North Fork Little River

The boundary line of the plantation is the same on both maps because the Barrow Plantation remained in the same family.

Plantation boundary

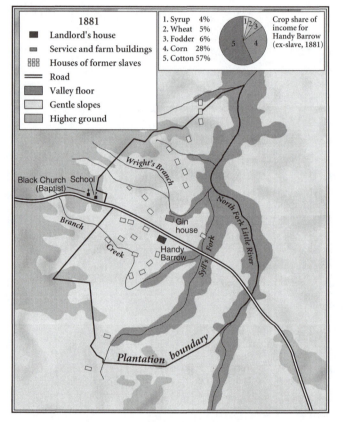

1881

- ■ Landlord's house
- ▭ Service and farm buildings
- ▦ Houses of former slaves
- ═ Road
- ▨ Valley floor
- ▢ Gentle slopes
- ▧ Higher ground

1. Syrup   4%
2. Wheat   5%
3. Fodder 6%
4. Corn   28%
5. Cotton 57%

Crop share of income for Handy Barrow (ex-slave, 1881)

Black Church (Baptist)   School

Wright's Branch

Branch Creek

Gin house

Handy Barrow

Syll's Fork

North Fork Little River

Plantation boundary

Maptalk

These maps attract the student of American history for a variety of reasons. First, they are large-scale maps in which the ratio of area on the maps to area on the ground is large enough to show individual features on the landscape: houses, schools, churches, and the like. Second, the maps are of interest because they show change over time. What was the impact of freedom on a community of slaves who became sharecroppers after emancipation? A popular magazine, *Scribner's Monthly,* raised this question in 1881. The pair of maps shown here first appeared as an illustration in that article. Third, students of history will also appreciate the notes on the map. These are often referred to as "call-outs," as if a guide were calling out explanations on a field trip.

One of the challenges of a large-scale map is to place the location into a larger geographical context. Sometimes this is done by an inset map, which indicates the featured location on a map of a much smaller scale. These maps do not have such a feature, but the names of the rivers are useful in establishing the Barrow Plantation's location.

Reading the Map

1. To establish a sense of the scale of this map, the house of the master or landlord is about three-fourths of a mile from Syll's Fork or about a mile and a quarter from the 1881 church.

2. The relative location of the Barrow Plantation is about 18 miles west of Washington, Georgia and about 12 miles north of today's Interstate Route 20, which connects Atlanta with Augusta.

3. These maps are oriented by the road, which generally runs north and south rather than by the cardinal directions. Thus east is at the top of this map and the North Fork of the Little River flows from the west to the east.

4. The Barrow Plantation is located in Oglethorpe County, named after the founder of Georgia.

5. Note that the maps show no houses immediately below (northwest of) Branch Creek. This low-lying area was covered with forest in 1860 as well as 1881, but soon thereafter a patch was cleared upstream along Syll's Fork to accommodate several new houses and fields.

Working with the Map

The changes recorded in the 1881 map probably did not happen at the same time. A third map, dated 1868 or 1870, might have recorded a transition from one pattern of settlement to another. Trace the major geographic features from one of these maps onto a new sheet of paper. Then develop a hypothetical map of the Barrow Plantation midway through the transition stage, say about 1869. Write two or three callouts for this new map explaining the changes in motion.

WORKSHEET 16
The Sioux Reservations in South Dakota

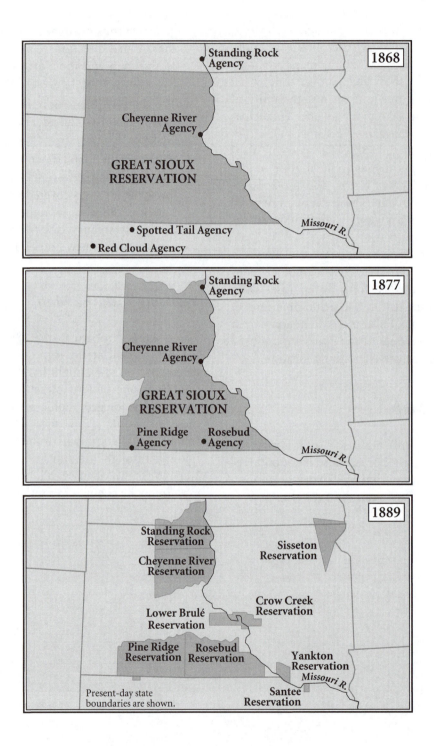

Maptalk

This sequence of three maps shows the constriction and fragmentation of Native American lands in South Dakota between 1868 and 1889. The word "reservation" in the map title is instructive and may be understood in several ways. In one sense, "to reserve" is to hold back. Historically, the U.S. government usually recognized that Native American groups had a prior claim to tribal lands. Therefore treaties had to be signed with the various tribes before the federal government could acquire a clear title to those lands. Only after a treaty did land become part of the public domain that could be sold, given way, or appropriated by the government. In the treaties, the tribes retained for their own use reserved lands that were not ceded.

"To reserve" also means to set apart or confine the use of a space to one particular person or group, as in "reserved seats" at performances. In this sense, a reservation could be considered something that is owned by the grantor and given to the grantee for some consideration. On the 1889 map the new reservations east of the Missouri River seem to be lands that the federal government had acquired and then granted to various groups of Native Americans. These might not have been a tribe's ancestral homes, but lands in another place given to a tribe in a treaty arrangement. Thus there seem to be two distinct types of reservation land on the 1889 map: ancestral lands and treaty-right lands. Ancestral lands were never ceded and thus belonged to the residents by tradition. Treaty-right lands once belonged to a different group of Native Americans but were acquired in a treaty with the United States.

Reading the Map

1. In the early nineteenth century the western Sioux, along with the Cheyennes, occupied a vast domain on the plains from Kansas northward, through South Dakota, to Canada.

2. The western Sioux peoples consisted of seven tribes, each of which was eventually confined by treaties to one of the reservations shown in the 1889 map.

3. In 1876, the year of Custer's "last stand," at the battle of Little Big Horn, the Sioux ceded the western strip of territory north of the Pine Ridge Agency shown on the second map.

4. In the 1880s, Native Americans ceded lands in the west-central part of the South Dakota territory to the U.S. government, followed in 1893, 1895, 1907, and 1911 by more cessions that are not indicated on this sequence of maps.

Working with the Map

As a young man of 18, Moses K. Armstrong worked as a surveyor in the Dakota region. In 1866 he published a book on the Black Hills and the Badlands west of the Missouri River, then homeland of the Sioux peoples. This was a region, he explained, "which has always excited the interest of geologists and explorers, but remains, even up to the present time [1866], a mysterious and underdeveloped belt of the continent where none but the wild beast and red man hold dominion." A few pages later, Armstrong expressed the belief that "the day is not far distant when a commercial city will spring up in the citadel of these hills of wealth which will direct the iron track of the first railway from the upper Mississippi to the northern mines of the Rocky Mountains" (from *The Early Empire Builders of the Great West,* pp. 44, 48).

Write a paragraph connecting Armstrong's prediction in 1866 with the tale told by these maps in the period 1868–89.

The Expansion of the Railroad System, 1870–1890

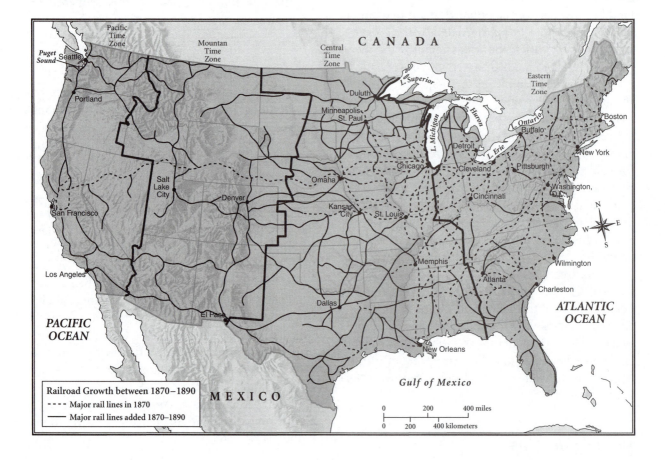

Maptalk

The necessary simplification of a map may mislead a reader in many ways. In the case of this map, the culprits are the word "system" and the fact that the same lines represent all tracks no matter their gauge (the width between rails). The word system is appropriate for 1890 because by that year all of the major lines used the same standard gauge so that the rolling stock of the railroad companies were interchangeable. In 1870, however, flexibility was rare.

Early railroads in the United States used at least four separate gauges. Each company used its own locomotives and cars. Gradually, shorter lines consolidated into longer lines adopting one standard gauge so that cars could be shuttled from one railroad to another.

In 1883, all the railroads agreed to follow standard times, another step in the emergence of a national system. The railroad companies divided the country into time zones where it would be the same time at every place in the designated area. Crossing into another zone, the clock would jump ahead or behind one hour. By eliminating the old "local time" for each station, the various lines could coordinate their schedules.

densely settled areas. The western lines, in contrast, had long routes across sparsely settled regions. The dividing line between the two types of railroads extended roughly from Chicago to New Orleans.

2. By 1870 Chicago emerged as the nation's great rail center where many eastern lines connected with their western counterparts. This network was one of the city's greatest assets, helping its economic recovery after the great fire of 1871.

3. In 1850 many observers expected St. Louis to become the railroad hub of the nation, but its focus on steamboat traffic and the disruption of the Civil War damaged its claim to railroad leadership. A bridge across the Mississippi at St. Louis was not completed until 1874.

4. El Paso was somewhat isolated until the arrival of the railroad in 1881. Until then, local carpenters and cabinetmakers made almost all of the furniture in El Paso. With the coming of the trains, however, manufactured furniture in the latest styles could be purchased at a modest cost. Suddenly wealthy and middle-class families rushed to furnish their homes in the fashionable "railroad way."

Reading the Map

1. A railroad executive looking at this map in 1890 would see two railroad systems. The eastern railroads had shorter lines serving

Working with the Map

Use a highlighter or a series of colored markers to trace the following routes on the map. Number them according to the table below.

Railroad	Route
1. Boston and Maine	Along the New England coast
2. Illinois Central	From Chicago to the mouth of the Ohio River
3. Union Pacific-Central Pacific	First transcontinental route; Omaha to San Francisco
4. Texas and Pacific	Dallas to El Paso
5. Great Northern	Duluth to Puget Sound
6. Southern Pacific	New Orleans to Los Angeles to San Francisco
7. Atlantic Coast Line	Washington, D.C. to Wilmington, N.C.

The Diffusion of the Australian Ballot

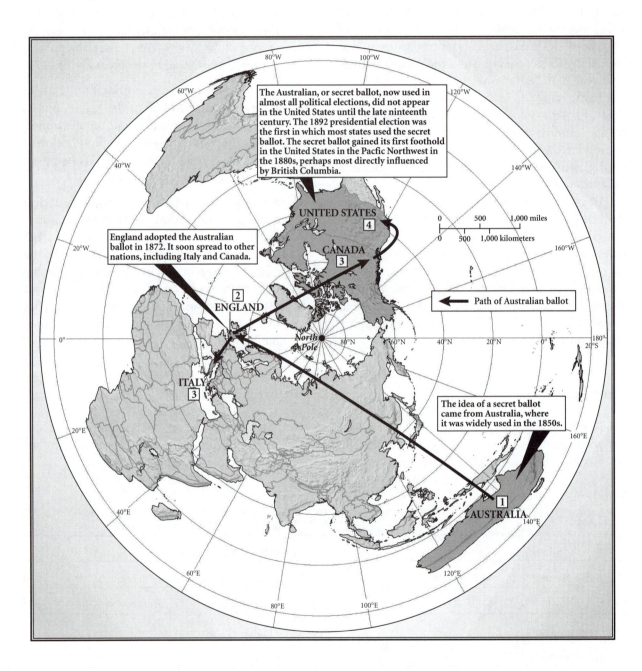

The Australian, or secret ballot, now used in almost all political elections, did not appear in the United States until the late ninteenth century. The 1892 presidential election was the first in which most states used the secret ballot. The secret ballot gained its first foothold in the United States in the Pacfic Northwest in the 1880s, perhaps most directly influenced by British Columbia.

England adopted the Australian ballot in 1872. It soon spread to other nations, including Italy and Canada.

The idea of a secret ballot came from Australia, where it was widely used in the 1850s.

← Path of Australian ballot

UNITED STATES 4

CANADA 3

ENGLAND 2

ITALY 3

AUSTRALIA 1

North Pole

0   500   1,000 miles
0   500   1,000 kilometers

Maptalk

This type of projection is not used often in historical work, but it is a good one for this map showing the paths of the Australian ballot to the United States. It is an Azimuthal equidistant projection, which means that every straight line that crosses the center point of the map is a great circle extending around the globe that marks off points of equal distance from the central point. Because the central point in this case is one of the poles, it is often called a polar projection.

Although real direction on the map is absolutely true only for one location, the North Pole, the image seems to bring the six inhabited continents close to one another. Australia is thus seen in a dynamic relationship to the rest of the globe rather than, as in the more familiar Mercator projection (see Worksheet A), relegated to a far-off corner at the bottom of a map.

The call-outs tell the story of the diffusion of the secret ballot; the significant places are numbered on the map in proper sequence. The nation states mentioned in the call-outs are prominently labeled and the other continents are marked with modern political boundaries to remind us that this map illustrates a political concept and that the Australian ballot eventually reached every Western nation.

Reading the Map

1. Azimuthal equidistant maps are often used in planning air routes because a straight line represents the shortest air route from the central place to any other place.

2. The straight lines on this image, from Australia to England, do not pass through the center of the map at the North Pole. Therefore they are not great circle routes and do not trace the shortest distance between these two points.

3. Note that the diffusion of the secret ballot in the United States generally followed a west to east pattern rather than the common east to west pattern of settlement and development.

4. The scale of distance is accurate only for great circle routes on the map. Therefore this scale cannot be used to measure the lines of diffusion.

5. A north-polar projection is a very effective tool to illustrate some essential facts about the world's oceans. It shows that the world's oceans are, in fact, a single great body of water joined around the North Pole and at the southern extremities of the map. Demonstrating that all the oceans are one body was a great achievement of the European age of exploration. The voyage around the globe by Ferdinand Magellan proved the one-ocean hypothesis in 1521–1522.

Working with the Map

For this exercise, use different colors to indicate the routes for the dissemination of the Australian ballot from Sydney, Australia, to Washington, D.C. For assistance, consult the maps in your textbook or a reference atlas. Label the following locations as you draw the routes. First, beginning in Sydney, trace around the south of Australia and across the Indian Ocean to the Red Sea. Then trace the route up the Red Sea, through the Suez Canal, across the Mediterranean Sea, touching Italy before passing the Strait of Gibraltar to reach England. From England, the Australian ballot crossed the North Atlantic Ocean to the Gulf of St. Lawrence and then west to reach Vancouver. From there the practice then entered the United States through Oregon and Washington. Use of the Australian ballot then proceeded eastward to the nation's capital city, Washington, D.C. Label these locations as well.

An additional line can be added to show a more direct path of diffusion from Sydney across the Pacific with a stop at Honolulu before entering the Juan de Fuca Strait to reach Vancouver.

The Lower East Side, New York City, 1900

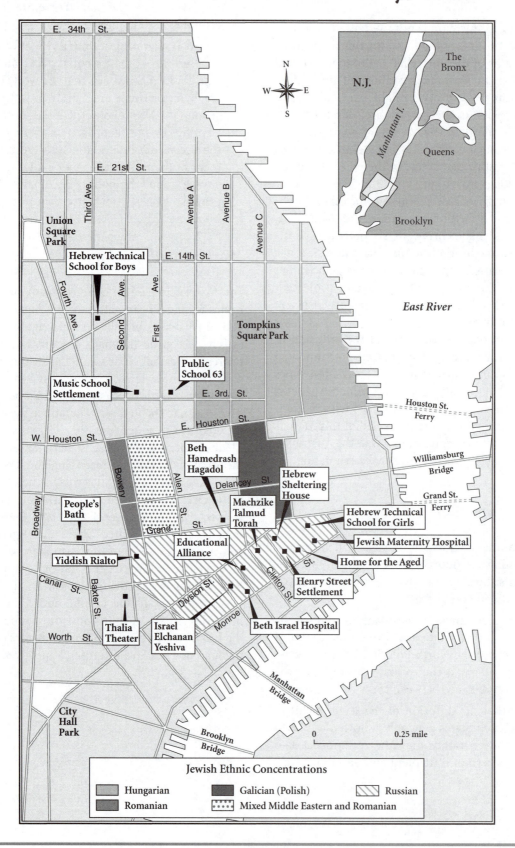

Maptalk

Place names often hold clues to local geography and the historical experience of a particular location. The Lower East Side, a section of New York City, is a good example. The inset location map at the top of the page shows the five major parts (boroughs) of New York. The Lower East Side, the main area of this map, is on the island of Manhattan. Manhattan extends north from New York harbor, with the Hudson River on the west and a strait called the East River on the east. The East River is actually an extension of Long Island Sound. Queens and Brooklyn are located at the western tip of Long Island. The Bronx is the only borough of New York located on the mainland, and is separated from Manhattan by the Harlem River, a diversion of the Hudson River that feeds some fresh water into the East River.

It is easy to see why the neighborhood featured here is called the East Side since it is situated on the eastern portion of the island fronting the East River. It gets the designation "Lower" because the Hudson River flows from the north to the south, the southern tip of Manhattan, where the Lower East Side is located, being at the end of its run.

The Lower East Side Tenement Museum tells the history of this neighborhood, reconstructing the kinds of nineteenth-century apartments that newly arrived immigrant families rented. Sometimes a dozen people squeezed into a one-room flat that rented for a dollar or two a month. Much of the heritage of this neighborhood centers on its role as a port-of-entry for immigrants. This map shows that various Jewish ethnic groups were a major component of the population.

Reading the Map

1. Two street patterns are shown on the map. The earliest, below Houston Street, is an irregular mix of streets following the lay of the land or paralleling the coastline.

2. North of Houston Street the entire island is dominated by a grid pattern of streets numbered in numerical order. The avenues generally run north-south and the streets run east-west.

3. Broadway is the major street running much of the length of the island. It follows a diagonal path across the grid because it was an important thoroughfare before the grid was established. Broadway's famous theater district is off this map to the north.

4. The Bowery has always been a major local commercial street for the Lower East Side and has been celebrated in many stories and songs.

Working with the Map

Using information provided on the map, develop two demographic charts showing different age groups in one column and several institutions that would be important to that particular cohort in the second column. Make one chart for males and another for females. Of course, some institutions will appeal to individuals across gender and age categories.

Male		Female	
Age Group	Institution	Age Group	Institution

Woman Suffrage, 1890–1919

Dates on the map indicate when individual states, on their own initiative, granted full suffrage to women.

Note how women won the right to vote in a roughly west to east movement. What reasons might be advanced to explain this pattern of diffusion?

CANADA

WASH.
1910

OREGON
1912

MONTANA
1914

NORTH
DAKOTA

MINN.

ME.

VT. N.H.

NEW
YORK
1917

MASS.

IDAHO
1896

WYOMING
1890

SOUTH
DAKOTA
1918

WIS.

MICH.
1918

R.I.

CONN.

N.J.

NEVADA
1914

UTAH
1896

COLORADO
1893

NEBRASKA

IOWA

ILL.

IND.

OHIO

PA.

DEL.

MD.

W.
VA.

VA.

CALIF.
1911

KANSAS
1912

MO.

KY.

NORTH
CAROLINA

ARIZONA
1912

NEW
MEXICO

OKLAHOMA
1918

ARK.

TENNESSEE

S.C.

PACIFIC
OCEAN

TEXAS

LA.

MISS.

ALA.

GEORGIA

ATLANTIC
OCEAN

FLA.

0   250   500 miles

0   250   500 kilometers

MEXICO

Effective Date of Equal Suffrage

By 1909

1910–1918

Partial suffrage by 1919

No woman suffrage by 1919

This map uses patterns and shades of gray to divide the states into four categories. **Polka dots** indicate where women had the right to vote before 1910. In **diagonally striped** states women had equal voting rights prior to 1919. **Light gray** shows where women enjoyed the right to vote in some elections, but not others. **Dark gray** indicates the states where women could not vote at all in 1919.

(after Opdycke)

Maptalk

Using a basic political map of the United States to illustrate the development of political movements is a common practice in history textbooks. The term "movement" is interesting and it always poses a cartographic challenge. With "move" as the root word, such maps always indicate change and they often tell a story divided into several parts. Thus these "movement" maps require the reader to envision change over time on a static piece of paper.

The states are usually the key subdivisions on a political map of the United States. In this example, state boundaries are the only geographical feature with the exception of three large inland lakes in Utah, Louisiana, or Florida. Because each state has its own constitution and government, the individual states often serve as laboratories for new political practices and institutions. One state might be venturesome and try out a new idea; later several others, often its neighbors, will adopt the practice. If successful, the idea might spread beyond the region and be adopted on a national level. The woman suffrage movement between 1890 and 1919 followed this pattern in classic fashion.

Reading the Map

1. Wyoming granted full suffrage to women in 1890, the first state to do so.

2. Within six years three neighboring states followed Wyoming's example, demonstrating the new practice to the rest of the nation.

3. Note that no state followed the example of the initial four in the next fourteen years. During this quiet period on the legislative front the proponents of woman suffrage organized nationally and advocated for change, often citing the example of the first four states.

4. Between 1910 and 1918, eight additional states contiguous to the first four adopted full woman's suffrage. California, then New York and Michigan, were the first "outlying" states to join the movement.

5. By the adoption in 1919 of the Nineteenth Amendment to the federal Constitution, almost all of the states in the West and Midwest had adopted partial woman's suffrage, paving the way for a smooth transition to national woman suffrage in the presidential election of 1920.

Working with the Map

Using your textbook or other reference book as a guide, write a caption in several sentences that outlines the progress of woman suffrage in the United States as illustrated by the map. In your caption, be sure to explain why states in the west granted women the right to vote earlier than those in the east.

The American Empire, 1917

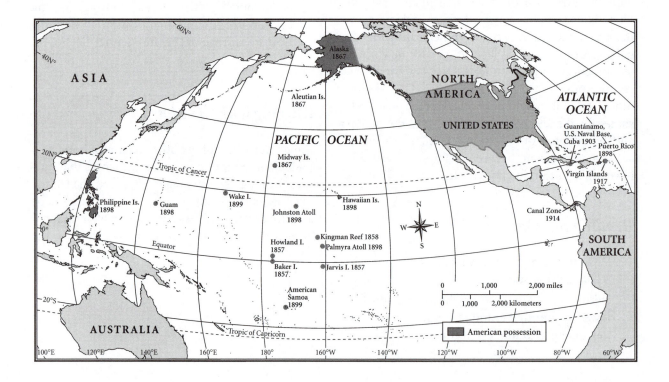

Maptalk

Thomas Jefferson once referred to the United States as an "empire for liberty." As president in the early nineteenth century, he enlarged this empire to continental proportions with the purchase of Louisiana in 1803. In the following decades, expansion of the national boundaries became a major theme of American history. Pausing during the Civil War, the movement resumed with the purchase of Alaska in 1867, and then became dormant until a burst of imperialism closed out the nineteenth century. The annexation of Hawaii and the Spanish-American War of 1898 extended the territorial expanse of the United States so that a map extending half of the way around the world is needed to show the extent of the U.S. empire in 1917.

This map is centered on the 160th west meridian that crosses the Alaska mainland, the Aleutian Islands, and the Hawaiian chain. It features the tropical portion of the Pacific Ocean. Note how almost all of the American possessions in 1917, except Alaska, are located between the tropics of Cancer and Capricorn. As a result of this focus of the map, the United States itself is pushed toward the margin of the pages. The west is emphasized, encouraging a Pacific outlook. This perspective, and this map, became familiar to Americans after the attack on Pearl Harbor in 1941. It remained a familiar image throughout the twentieth century with the economic development of East Asian nations in the post-World War II decades.

Reading the Map

1. If the reader looks at this map in terms of population rather than area, the Philippine Islands support many more people than all of the rest of the U.S. Pacific possessions combined. Gained as a result of the Spanish-American War beginning in 1898, an American presence off the coast of Asia made the United States a major player in the affairs of the Far East.

2. By 1917 Alaska attracted the nation's attention because of several significant discoveries of gold and other mineral resources in the previous decades. Miners and the fishing industry supported regular ocean connections between Seattle and stations in Alaska.

3. In 1917 many strategic locations in the American empire were coaling stations on small islands scattered across the Pacific. Both naval vessels and commercial steamships used these stations to extend their reach.

4. The most strategic place on the map, however, would soon be the Canal Zone where the Panama Canal facilitated seaborne commerce between Atlantic and Pacific ports. Completed in 1914, the canal also permitted ships sailing between Asia and Europe to cut through the Americas, a significant stimulus to world trade.

Working with the Map

An informed viewer of this map will be able to locate the major ports on the West Coast of North America as well as in East Asia. Use a world map to check these locations, and then record the following on the map.

North American Ports	Overseas Ports
San Francisco	Manila
Seattle	Hong Kong
Portland	Tokyo
Los Angeles	Sidney
San Diego	Shanghai
Vancouver	Honolulu
Anchorage	

Use colored lines to mark the diamond-shaped American sphere of interest in the North Pacific Ocean by connecting the following ports:

San Francisco and Honolulu

San Francisco and Anchorage

Anchorage and Manila

Manila and Honolulu

Manila and Samoa

Samoa and San Francisco

Anchorage and Samoa

In a brief paragraph, write a policy statement on American interests in the Pacific for the year 1917.

WORKSHEET 22

World War I: U.S. Participation on the Western Front, 1918

Legend:
- Major battles involving U.S. forces
- Allied offensive
- Territory under German control by July 1918
- Line of trench warfare, 1915–1917
- Armistice line, November 11, 1918

Maptalk

With the exception of the American Revolution and the War of 1812, virtually all the foreign wars involving the United States have taken place outside the nation's borders. America's involvement in battles during the First World War is shown here on a map of Western Europe. Almost the entire American effort was concentrated on the Western Front, and this map focuses on the frontier between Germany and France and the small nation of Belgium sandwiched in between the two.

The dramatic arrows on the map highlight the shift of the front lines eastward as American troops attacked enemy positions beginning in May 1918. The dates on the map show that the German army was pushed back very slowly, less than 50 miles in 18 months. Looked at another way, in about 540 days (18 months) the Allies gained about 88,000 yards (50 miles), an average of less than 165 yards a day.

Reading the Map

1. The agonizingly slow movement of the front lines on the Western Front was accompanied by huge numbers of battlefield casualties, a fact hidden by the smooth flow of the graphics on the map.

2. The arrows all point in one direction, which records the overall flow of battle. Many interim reverses, hesitations, and irregularities are hidden underneath these generalized arrows. The German armies, for example, made major drives west between March and July 1918.

3. Note how the line of trench warfare, 1915–1917, extends from the North Sea to the border of neutral Switzerland. More mobile warfare did, of course, continue on the high seas throughout these years.

4. Fighting occurred on other fronts. The Eastern Front, where Russian troops contested German advances, ended with the Communist Revolution of 1917 and the withdrawal of Soviet forces from the fighting. As German troops moved from the Eastern to the Western Front, the Americans arrived to balance the massing of German forces.

Working with the Map

Use a photocopy of the world physical geography outline map found in the Appendix to put the Western Front in the context of the global reach of World War I. Consult your textbook and/or an historical atlas and indicate the following locations.

1. The area covered by this map of the Western Front

2. The Eastern Front as finally set by the Treaty of Brest-Litovsk between Russia and the Central Powers, March 1918, extended from the Gulf of Finland to the mouth of the Don River at the Sea of Azov. Draw this line on your map.

3. The Italian front saw fierce fighting after Italy declared war on Austria-Hungary in May 1915. Eleven major offensives launched by Italy gained little territory at a high human cost. Mark this area on your map.

4. Other campaigns during World War I occurred in the German territories in Africa, in Turkey and the Near East, on the Balkan Peninsula, and in China. Mark these areas on your map:

   a. Dar es Salaam: British troops land to attack German forces, August 1914

   b. Belgrade: a combined German-Austrian-Bulgarian army crosses the Danube River to invade Serbia, October 1915

   c. The Battle of Jutland fought on the North Sea

   d. Jerusalem: captured by the British from the Turks, December 1917

The Shift from Rural to Urban Population, 1920–1930

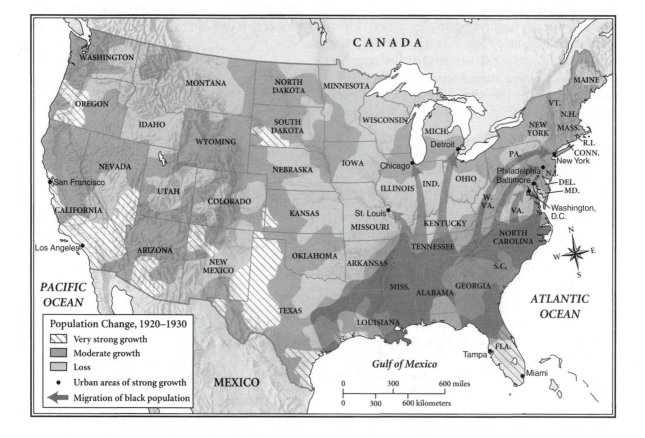

Population Change, 1920–1930
- Very strong growth
- Moderate growth
- Loss
- • Urban areas of strong growth
- ← Migration of black population

Maptalk

Three distinct factors inform us that this is a dynamic map featuring change over time. First are the bold arrows indicating the Great Migration of African Americans from the rural South to the urban North and West. Next, the shading on the map shows population changes—very strong population growth, moderate growth, or a net loss of population in the 1920s. Finally, the prominent black dots indicate urban areas that showed marked population increases over the same decade.

The reader is challenged to identify the various elements of the population change shown on the map. Once these movements are understood, one should try to relate them to each other or to broad historical trends. Population changes may be caused by two factors: (1) any variation from an equal number of births and deaths, and (2) the movement of people. Obviously, if the number of births exceeds the number of deaths, population will increase if no one moves away. Conversely, if the number of births is less than the number of deaths, and no one moves in, the population of place will decline.

But people are always on the move, especially in a mobile society like the United States. Changes of residence can be short moves across town or long migrations across the nation. If movement crosses state lines, it will be recorded on maps, such as this one, that are based on census data. This type of move is often called internal migration. Newcomers entering the nation with the intention of taking up permanent residence in the United States are immigrants.

Reading the Map

1. Two important factors contributed to strong to moderate population growth in the 1920s along both coastal regions. Immigrants often settled in or near their original ports of entry.

Also, as the nation industrialized, areas with good port cities possessed advantages as sites for manufacturing, warehousing, and distribution facilities, attracting workers.

2. Almost all of the rapidly growing cities in the Northeast became destinations for black migrants from the rural South.

3. Mechanization transformed the nation's farms in the 1920s. The rapid adoption of gasoline-powered tractors displaced horses, and farms thus needed fewer workers. This change is reflected in the loss of population in many agricultural regions.

4. California experienced a major growth spurt in the 1920s, accounting for about 12 percent of the nation's total population increase in that decade.

5. New York State also recorded a huge jump in population during the 1920s, adding over two million residents, slightly fewer than California.

Working with the Map

Statistics often help a reader put a map like this one into focus. Record the actual changes in population on the map for the following states. (Subtracting the census figures for 1920 from those for 1930 generated the data.)

1. California	+ 2,250,039
2. New York	+ 2,202,839
3. Texas	+ 1,161,223
4. Illinois	+ 1,145,374
5. Missouri	+ 225,312
6. Kansas	+ 111,742
7. Montana	– 11,283

The Dust Bowl, 1930–1941

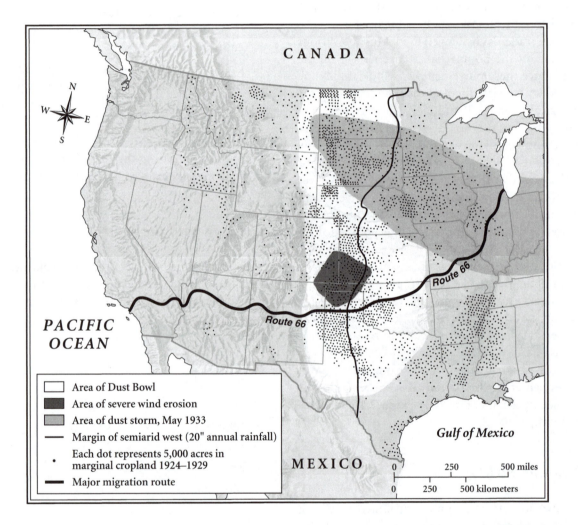

CANADA

N W E S

PACIFIC OCEAN

Route 66

Route 66

MEXICO

Gulf of Mexico

Area of Dust Bowl
Area of severe wind erosion
Area of dust storm, May 1933
Margin of semiarid west (20" annual rainfall)
Each dot represents 5,000 acres in marginal cropland 1924–1929
Major migration route

0   250   500 miles
0   250   500 kilometers

Maptalk

Weather maps are very common and are found every day in newspapers, television reports, and on the Internet, but *climate* maps are not widely used or commonly understood.

Climate is the sum of weather conditions in any given location over a long period of time, perhaps centuries. The two essential elements of a climate are temperature and precipitation. The average range of temperature as well as the amount and pattern of precipitation divide the year into seasons. Variations of temperature and precipitation from time to time also shape the nature of climate. There is an element of predictability in every climate, but extremes often have great impact on human activities.

This map illustrates the tragic results for some Americans who failed to consider climatic patterns. Extreme dryness in mid-America led to the Dust Bowl in the 1930s. A succession of wet years in the 1920s had encouraged farmers to plow up pastures for cropland, but at the end of the decade the pattern of high precipitation quickly changed and a series of very dry years produced an intense drought. After the grasses died, winds picked up the parched topsoil and carried it away as dust. Farmers abandoned drought-stricken states and searched for places of greater economic opportunities. The circumstances of the Great Depression, however, placed severe limits on the migrants. The result was a human tragedy and ecological disaster.

Reading the Map

1. The high plains extending north from Texas mark the border between wet America to the east and dry or arid America to the west. The exact boundary shifts over time, westward in dry seasons and eastward in wet years.

2. The great dust storm of May 1933 darkened the skies above St. Louis, Chicago, Indianapolis, and cities all the way to the Atlantic.

3. The greatest impact of the drought centered on western Oklahoma. Severe erosion wore away fields and moved the soil in dune-like forms that buried houses, barns, and even whole settlements.

4. Route 66, a newly improved U.S. highway from Chicago to Los Angeles, provided a convenient escape route from the devastated panhandle areas of Oklahoma and Texas. Most people fled west to California, but many also tried their luck in cities to the east, like Chicago.

Working with the Map

Route 66 first appeared on maps in 1927. A numbering system for U.S. highways, approved in 1926, assigned the number 66 to the highway connecting the Great Lakes with southern California. Early tourist maps called Route 66 the "Main Street of America." Consult a reference atlas to locate the following places on the map:

1. Chicago was the start of the highway.

2. St. Louis was the highway's crossing of the Mississippi River.

3. Joplin, Missouri was famous for its entertainment district in the 1930s, largely because the states of Kansas and Oklahoma to the west were "dry" (here, meaning alcohol free) states.

4. Tulsa, Oklahoma, called itself the "Oil Capital of the World" on 1930s postcards.

5. In Amarillo, Texas, the Federal Emergency Relief Administration set up the Transient Bureau to help people who wanted to leave the Dust Bowl.

6. Albuquerque, New Mexico, marked the place where the highway crossed the Rio Grande.

7. Flagstaff, Arizona, was located near the snow-capped San Francisco peaks.

8. At Needles, California, the road crossed the Colorado River.

9. Los Angeles was the goal of many travelers, who often ran across the beach at Santa Monica to splash into the Pacific Ocean as soon as they arrived.

Eleanor Roosevelt's Travels, 1936–1937

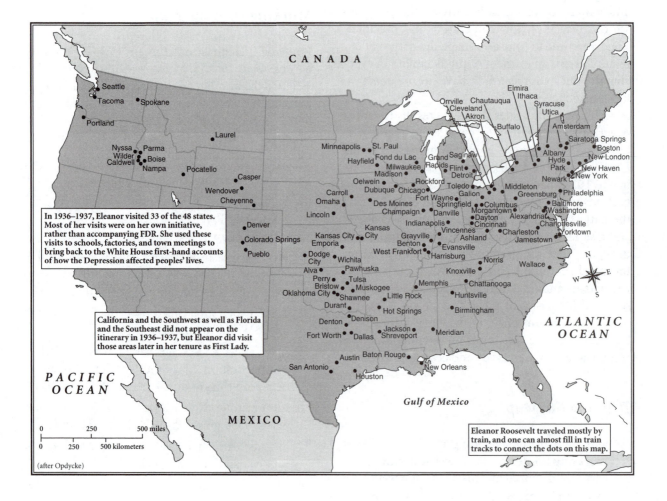

In 1936–1937, Eleanor visited 33 of the 48 states. Most of her visits were on her own initiative, rather than accompanying FDR. She used these visits to schools, factories, and town meetings to bring back to the White House first-hand accounts of how the Depression affected peoples' lives.

California and the Southwest as well as Florida and the Southeast did not appear on the itinerary in 1936–1937, but Eleanor did visit those areas later in her tenure as First Lady.

Eleanor Roosevelt traveled mostly by train, and one can almost fill in train tracks to connect the dots on this map.

(after Opdycke)

Maptalk

This is at once a personal and a political map. It shows the places President Franklin Roosevelt's wife, Eleanor Roosevelt, visited in her role as First Lady in 1936 and 1937. It does not show the routes she took to reach these places and no dates are given for specific visits. If you were to draw a personal map of your movements over a two-year period you might want to show both the routes you took as well as the dates of travel. In this case, however, the cartographer has omitted this information so that the reader can concentrate on one essential point: the First Lady visited a huge number of places when representing her husband's administration.

Reading the Map

1. Eleanor Roosevelt bypassed a dozen states during 1936 and 1937. Two of these were in New England, two were on the northern plains, three were in the Southeast and five were in the Southwest.

2. Note how the placement of the call-outs tends to hide the fact that Roosevelt's travels did not include the Southwest in 1936–1937.

3. One can almost trace the railroad tracks along the Front Range of the Rocky Mountains in Colorado and Wyoming by connecting the city dots on this map.

4. At this time most interstate travel was by rail, a fact suggested in several places by the map. For example, note the string of places visited in Ohio, the dots along the rail corridor between Washington and Boston, and those marking the Snake River in Idaho and Oregon.

Working with the Map

Use the map to determine which of the following large cities received an "official" visit by the First Lady in 1936 or 1937. Record your findings on the chart below.

City	Visited	Not Visited
New York		
Chicago		
Los Angeles		
Philadelphia		
Detroit		
San Francisco		
Baltimore		
Boston		
Cleveland		
New Orleans		
St. Louis		
Pittsburgh		
Cincinnati		
Kansas City		
Buffalo		
Dallas		

WORKSHEET 26

World War II in the North Atlantic, 1939–1943

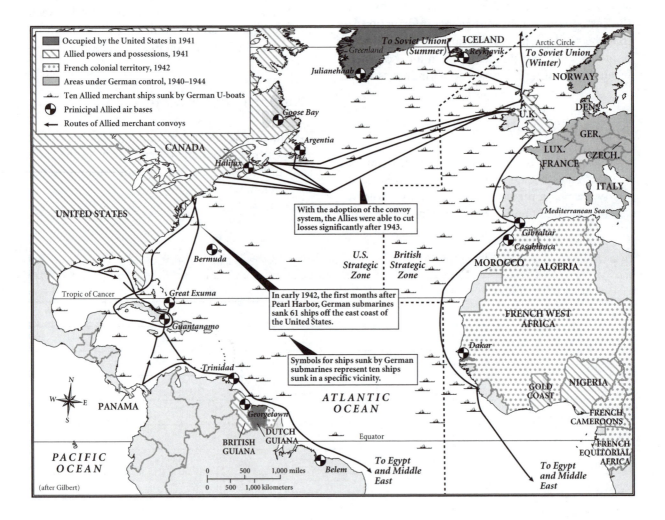

Legend:
- Occupied by the United States in 1941
- Allied powers and possessions, 1941
- French colonial territory, 1942
- Areas under German control, 1940–1944
- Ten Allied merchant ships sunk by German U-boats
- Principal Allied air bases
- Routes of Allied merchant convoys

With the adoption of the convoy system, the Allies were able to cut losses significantly after 1943.

In early 1942, the first months after Pearl Harbor, German submarines sank 61 ships off the east coast of the United States.

Symbols for ships sunk by German submarines represent ten ships sunk in a specific vicinity.

To Soviet Union (Summer)
To Soviet Union (Winter)

ICELAND — Reykjavik
Greenland
Julianehaab
Goose Bay
Argentia
Halifax
CANADA
UNITED STATES
Bermuda
Tropic of Cancer
Great Exuma
Guantanamo
PANAMA
Trinidad
Georgetown
BRITISH GUIANA
DUTCH GUIANA
Belem
PACIFIC OCEAN
ATLANTIC OCEAN
Equator
To Egypt and Middle East

U.S. Strategic Zone
British Strategic Zone

Arctic Circle
NORWAY
DEN.
U.K.
GER.
LUX.
FRANCE
CZECH.
ITALY
Mediterranean Sea
Gibraltar
Casablanca
MOROCCO
ALGERIA
FRENCH WEST AFRICA
Dakar
GOLD COAST
NIGERIA
FRENCH CAMEROONS
FRENCH EQUITORIAL AFRICA
To Egypt and Middle East

N W E S

0   500   1,000 miles
0   500   1,000 kilometers

(after Gilbert)

Maptalk

A map of the Atlantic Ocean is an important tool for understanding American history. This is certainly true of the era of European exploration, of the colonial period, of the wars in the eighteenth century for empire and independence, of the African diaspora, of the story of immigration, and, in this case, of the great world wars of the twentieth century. In historical maps, land usually forms the focal point. Here it is the sea that takes the center stage. Four continents border the Atlantic Ocean, along with the islands of Greenland and Iceland at the north.

The symbols designating the ships sunk by German submarines and the routes of Allied convoys guarding merchant ships dominate the ocean's surface on this map, but an informed eye will also note the geographical construction of the North Atlantic. This projection starts with the equator at the bottom, which runs from just above Belem in Brazil to Africa. The Tropic of Cancer runs parallel to this line, cutting through the Straits of Florida north of Cuba. The Arctic Circle, another parallel, cuts across Greenland and touches the northernmost point of Iceland.

The Gulf Stream, a river of warm water in the ocean, leaves the Straits of Florida as a strong current and pushes northeasterly across the Atlantic Ocean until it reaches the British Isles, moderating the climate of Western Europe. Thus Goose Bay, Labrador, is much colder than Liverpool in the United Kingdom at about the same latitude.

Reading the Map

1. At the outbreak of the war in Europe in 1939, German military leaders calculated that if they could sink 750,000 tons of shipping bound for Britain each month, they could knock the U.K. out of the war. The war at sea became a critical arena in the early years of the war. Note the concentration of U-boat activity at the western approaches to the British Isles.

2. Between September 1939 and June 1941, the German navy sunk almost 1800 merchant ships on the high seas. It was an astounding number, but never reached a figure high enough to force a British surrender.

3. Control of shipping space and a strict system of rationing reduced British import needs. But it was the convoy system, fully implemented by the end of 1941, which enabled the British to withstand the German assault.

4. The destruction of merchant ships by German submarines continued to the end of the war and expanded to the South Atlantic, the Indian, and the Pacific Oceans.

Working with the Map

This exercise provides the opportunity to familiarize yourself with the geography of World War II in its Atlantic context. Please match the following places with the correct description.

_____ 1. Guantanamo A. Territory hosting Allied air base at Dakar

_____ 2. France B. Allied air base in Iceland

_____ 3. Morocco C. Allied air base in Canada

_____ 4. Greenland D. Allied air base located south of the Equator

_____ 5. French West Africa E. Allied air base located between the Equator and the Tropic of Cancer

_____ 6. Halifax F. French colonial territory and host of Allied air base at Casablanca

_____ 7. Reykjavik G. Westernmost nation under German control

_____ 8. Gibraltar H. German-occupied nation extending north of the Arctic Circle

_____ 9. Belem I. Allied-occupied nation with an air base at Julianehaab

_____ 10. Norway J. Allied air base at the strategic entrance of the Mediterranean Sea

American Global Defense Treaties in the Cold War Era

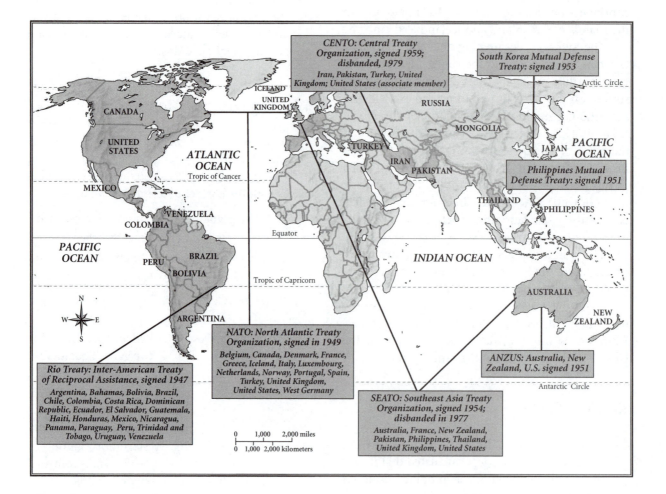

CENTO: Central Treaty Organization, signed 1959; disbanded, 1979

Iran, Pakistan, Turkey, United Kingdom; United States (associate member)

South Korea Mutual Defense Treaty: signed 1953

Philippines Mutual Defense Treaty: signed 1951

NATO: North Atlantic Treaty Organization, signed in 1949

Belgium, Canada, Denmark, France, Greece, Iceland, Italy, Luxembourg, Netherlands, Norway, Portugal, Spain, Turkey, United Kingdom, United States, West Germany

ANZUS: Australia, New Zealand, U.S. signed 1951

Rio Treaty: Inter-American Treaty of Reciprocal Assistance, signed 1947

Argentina, Bahamas, Bolivia, Brazil, Chile, Colombia, Costa Rica, Dominican Republic, Ecuador, El Salvador, Guatemala, Haiti, Honduras, Mexico, Nicaragua, Panama, Paraguay, Peru, Trinidad and Tobago, Uruguay, Venezuela

SEATO: Southeast Asia Treaty Organization, signed 1954; disbanded in 1977

Australia, France, New Zealand, Pakistan, Philippines, Thailand, United Kingdom, United States

Maptalk

A world map is needed to illustrate the Cold War and the extent of the formal defense pacts signed by the United States during this time. Actually, this example is not a full world map because the mid-Pacific region is cut off, as is Hawaii. The cartographer has also adjusted the map in other ways. The Prime Meridian is not exactly at the center of the image, nor is the equator. The lines of latitude and longitude have been omitted so as to avoid calling attention to this "decentering" of a familiar projection.

Because this is a political map, place names and boundary lines refer to nation-states. The continent of Antarctica need not be indicated because it is, by treaties, not permanently occupied by any nation. Only a few nations are identified on the map, and these are all (except Russia and Mongolia) signatories to one of the U.S. defense treaties.

Because all of the meridians on this map except the central one are curved toward the poles, the directions to the north and south change from place to place on the map. The parallels, however, are all straight lines so that lines due east and west always follow the top and bottom borders of the image.

Reading the Map

1. Russia is labeled on the map but the other republics of the Soviet Union are not. Kazakhstan and Ukraine were part of the USSR and are given separate boundaries, but they are not labeled.

2. Mongolia, between Russia and China, was a dependent state tied to the USSR but never officially part of the Soviet Union.

3. During the period 1945–1980, many former colonies in Africa and South Asia became independent nations. They are outlined on the map but not labeled because they represent most of the "third world" of nations aligned with neither the United States nor Soviet Union in the Cold War.

4. Note that the United States was a member of all of these defense arrangements, even though it is not listed in the call-outs listing the members of each pact.

5. Several European nations remained officially neutral throughout the Cold War, signing neither the NATO Treaty nor the Warsaw Pact of communist allies. These included Sweden, Finland, Ireland, Switzerland, Austria, and Yugoslavia.

Working with the Map

The communist bloc was led by the USSR and included both China and Mongolia from the beginning. After 1960 China pursued an independent but often parallel course with the Soviets. Mongolia remained dependent on the USSR throughout the Cold War. Color these communist bloc areas red on the map. The non-aligned nations at one time included almost all of Africa, India, Indonesia, and several adjacent nations. Color these areas green on the map. Use blue to show the U.S. and its defense partners in NATO, the Rio Pact, and ANZUS.

Next write a paragraph to serve as a caption for the map pointing out several locations where the Cold War turned into hot combat between 1945 and 1980.

The Interstate Highway System, 1930 and 1970

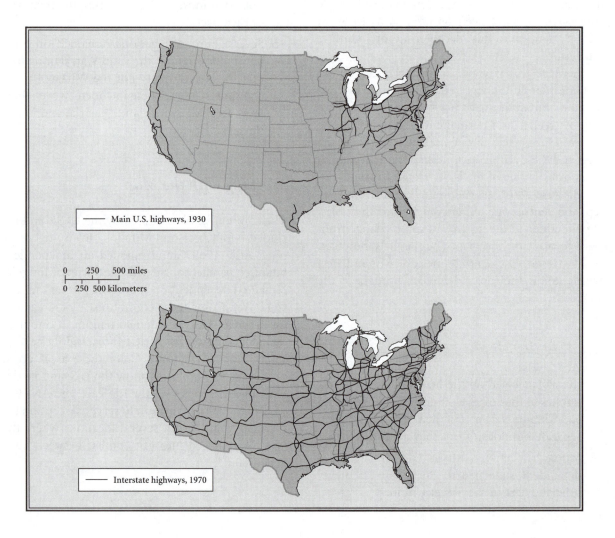

Main U.S. highways, 1930

0   250   500 miles

0   250   500 kilometers

Interstate highways, 1970

Maptalk

Highway maps are perhaps the most common type of American map. They can be found in the glove compartment of almost every car. In an automobile age, travelers consult them frequently, but road maps have a long history going back more than a century before the first automobiles.

There are two maps here, each representing a different year in the twentieth century. Only a student of history, it seems, would want an old highway map if an up-to-date map is available. In the early twentieth century, it was often difficult for motorists to find their way using an outdated map because the road pattern was in constant flux. A variety of local systems were used to designate routes until the standard U.S. highway numbers appeared in 1926.

Little of the Interstate Highway System existed before the National Defense Highway Act was passed in 1956 at the urging of President Dwight D. Eisenhower. The interstate highways quickly became major markers by which Americans connected the image on the map with the actual lay of the land. Seemingly overnight, motor routes became the primary geographical reference points for modern American society.

Reading the Map

1. Both maps simplify a complex situation. The 1930 example shows only completed four-lane highways, but omits many short stretches under construction. The 1970 map shows the entire Interstate system as it would be when it was completed. Not until 1978, however, was over 90 percent of the Interstates open to traffic.

2. Note that U.S. 66 was just being built in 1930. Only the section between Chicago and St. Louis shows up on the map. A Chicago-Los Angeles trip using the Interstate system in 1970 could follow several different combinations of routes.

3. On both the U.S. highways of 1930 and the Interstate system of 1970, even numbers generally indicated east-west routes while odd numbers designated north-south roads.

4. The goal of highway engineers was to have each state in the Interstate system served by at least one even numbered and one odd numbered highway. Does the 1970 map suggest that they were successful?

5. Although Hawaii later received some interstate-type highways, both the islands and Alaska were omitted from the 1970 system. By definition, isolated states could not have an interstate highway, a road *between* states.

Working with the Map

Please fill in the blanks with the correct answers. Consult a reference atlas to help locate specific places.

On the 1930 map there were (1)＿＿＿＿＿ main highways connecting California's two leading cities, (2)＿＿＿＿＿ and (3)＿＿＿＿＿. Note that one of the early major automobile roads in Texas reached north from the mouth of the (4)＿＿＿＿＿. By 1930 Florida had two major north-south highways in place, one, along the Atlantic coast, led from (5)＿＿＿＿＿ in the north to (6)＿＿＿＿＿ near the tip of the peninsula. Chicago, at the end of Lake (7)＿＿＿＿＿ seemed to be emerging as a highway hub following its role as the nation's leading railroad center.

The 1970 map shows (8)＿＿＿＿＿ Interstate highway routes crossing the Great Plains along the 100th Meridian. The northernmost route extends east from the state of Washington, and swings way to the south to cut through the city of (9)＿＿＿＿＿ as it runs around the (10)＿＿＿＿＿ lakes. Then it heads north again, eventually running alongside the Erie Canal in the state of (11)＿＿＿＿＿.

In the middle of the nation several Interstate hubs stand out on the map: (12)＿＿＿＿＿, at the Front Range of the Rocky Mountains, and (13)＿＿＿＿＿, the capital of the Oklahoma. The capital cities of Tennessee and Georgia also appear as motor hubs, (14)＿＿＿＿＿ and (15)＿＿＿＿＿ respectively.

The Vietnam War, 1954–1975

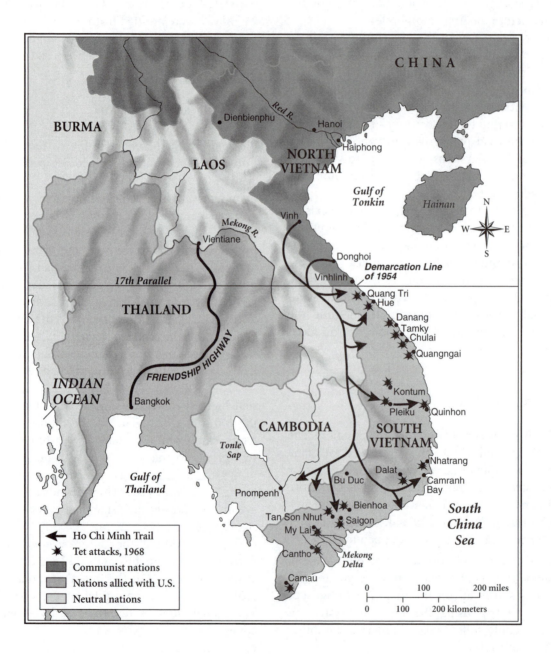

CHINA

BURMA

Dienbienphu

Red R.

Hanoi

Haiphong

LAOS

NORTH
VIETNAM

*Gulf of
Tonkin*

Hainan

N

W   E

S

Mekong R.

Vinh

Vientiane

Donghoi

17th Parallel

Vinhlinh

**Demarcation Line
of 1954**

THAILAND

Quang Tri
Hue

Danang
Tamky
Chulai

Quangngai

FRIENDSHIP HIGHWAY

INDIAN
OCEAN

Kontum

Bangkok

Pleiku   Quinhon

CAMBODIA

SOUTH
VIETNAM

*Tonle
Sap*

Nhatrang

Dalat

Camranh
Bay

*Gulf of
Thailand*

Bu Duc

*South
China
Sea*

Pnompenh

Bienhoa

Tan Son Nhut   Saigon

My Lai

Cantho   *Mekong
Delta*

Camau

	Ho Chi Minh Trail
	Tet attacks, 1968
	Communist nations
	Nations allied with U.S.
	Neutral nations

0   100   200 miles

0   100   200 kilometers

Maptalk

As in the case of the two world wars of the twentieth century, the maps used to illustrate America's involvement in the hot clashes of the Cold War led us overseas: first to Korea and then to Indochina, peninsulas jutting out from Asia into the Pacific Ocean. In both cases, the world's leading powers used major parallels to divide nations formerly united but pulled apart in the Cold War. In Korea, the 38th parallel was (and remains) used. In Vietnam, the 17th parallel served as a boundary from 1954 to 1975, until reunification under communist rule. The former was in the middle latitudes, about the same distance north as St. Louis or San Francisco Bay. The 17th parallel, however, is in the tropics, well south of Hawaii. The 17th parallel crosses Africa near Timbuktu and the Americas near Mexico's southern boundary.

South Vietnam, where the battles are marked on the map, has a hot, wet climate supporting lush tropical vegetation. The Mekong Delta is one vast tropical wetland, much of it turned into rice paddies. In the higher elevations, the vegetation cover thins out somewhat, and necessitated the use of different military tactics and weaponry.

Reading the Map

1. Note how the Mekong River makes a long journey from its source in China to its delta in then South Vietnam.
2. The "Friendship Highway" provided landlocked Laos with access to the ocean via Thailand, a nation allied with the United States.

3. The Ho Chi Minh Trail, named after the leader of North Vietnam, was a series of hidden routes along which military forces, equipment, and supplies could be sent from the north to various battlefields in the south. It cut through rugged regions and dense forests in the backcountry of two neutral nations: Laos and Cambodia.
4. The Ho Chi Minh Trail enabled Viet Cong forces, fighting against South Vietnamese and American troops, to mount surprise attacks in many locations during the Tet offensive of 1968.

Working with the Map

Please match the following places with the correct description:

_____ 1. Gulf of Tonkin

_____ 2. Bangkok

_____ 3. Hanoi

_____ 4. Saigon

_____ 5. Pnompenh

_____ 6. Hainan

_____ 7. Burma

_____ 8. Hue

A. Capital of North Vietnam

B. Capital of South Vietnam

C. City on the Mekong River

D. Island province of China

E. Nation on the Indian Ocean

F. Surrounded by North Vietnam and China

G. Battle site near the 17th parallel

H. Capital of Thailand

States Ratifying the Equal Rights Amendment, 1972–1977

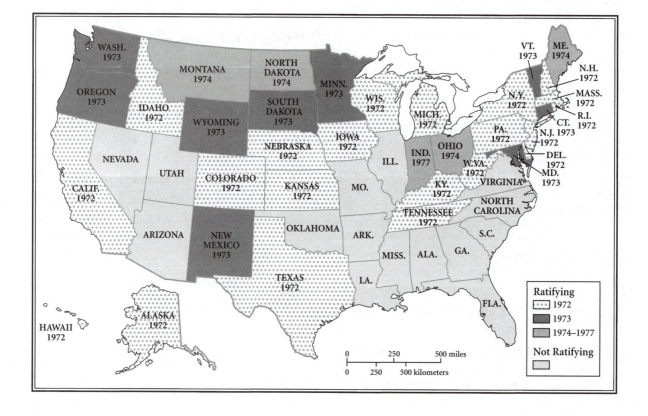

WASH. 1973

MONTANA 1974

NORTH DAKOTA 1974

MINN. 1973

VT. 1973

ME. 1974

N.H. 1972

OREGON 1973

IDAHO 1972

WYOMING 1973

SOUTH DAKOTA 1973

WIS. 1972

MICH. 1972

N.Y. 1972

MASS. 1972

R.I. 1972

CT. 1972

NEVADA

UTAH

NEBRASKA 1972

IOWA 1972

ILL.

IND. 1977

OHIO 1974

PA. 1972

N.J. 1973

DEL. 1972

CALIF. 1972

COLORADO 1972

KANSAS 1972

MO.

W.VA. 1972

KY. 1972

VIRGINIA

MD. 1973

ARIZONA

NEW MEXICO 1973

OKLAHOMA

ARK.

TENNESSEE 1972

NORTH CAROLINA

S.C.

TEXAS 1972

LA.

MISS.

ALA.

GA.

FLA.

HAWAII 1972

ALASKA 1972

Ratifying	
	1972
	1973
	1974–1977
Not Ratifying	

0   250   500 miles

0   250   500 kilometers

Maptalk

To show the entire United States in the 1970s, a composite of three separate maps of varying scale is used: one of the continental United States, the forty-eight contiguous states; a second at a smaller scale for Alaska; and then a third at a larger scale for Hawaii.

From a different perspective, this figure resembles a chart more than a map because the spatial dimensions are less important than the fact of how each state voted. However, a map is better than a simple chart of the votes because it encourages readers to start asking important "why" questions. The presentation on a map of how each state voted on the ERA suggests that geography might be part of the answer when analyzing the vote.

Reading the Map

1. In early 1972, the House of Representatives passed the Equal Rights Amendment (ERA) by a vote of 354 to 12. In March, the Senate followed suit with a vote of 84 to 8. The amendment allowed seven years for ratification, and the Constitution requires the approval of three-quarters (38) of the states to become law. Before the end of 1972, 22 states had voted for passage.

2. Eight additional states supported the ERA in 1973, but then the movement stalled, only five additional states voting for the amendment before the deadline.

3. The states that did not ratify the amendment fell into three groups. The South, the states of the former Confederacy with the exception of Texas, all rejected the ERA. Kentucky and Tennessee, which had been among the first states to ratify, later rescinded their vote, a move of questionable legality.

4. The second group of non-ratifying states were those with large Mormon populations like Utah and Idaho. The Mormon church opposed the ERA, holding that men and women had different roles in life. While Utah rejected the ERA, Idaho voted initially for the amendment, only to later rescind its support.

5. Illinois and Missouri fell into a third category: states which dragged their feet on ratification until Phyllis Schlafly of Illinois, a vigorous opponent, could win support for her "Stop ERA" movement.

Working with the Map

Use the nine Census Regions to analyze how each responded to the Equal Rights Amendment. (see Worksheet G on page 15) After completing the chart below, explain why you think the amendment failed to be ratified. How can we account for the strong resistance to the ERA in the South?

Census Region	States Ratifying	States Not Ratifying
New England		
Middle Atlantic		
South Atlantic		
East North Central		
West North Central		
East South Central		
West South Central		
Mountain		
Pacific		

The Collapse of Communism in Eastern Europe and the Soviet Union, 1989–1991

Maptalk

This is an unusual map to conclude a series of maps on American history. The United States is absent. Why?

In 1989, Francis Fukuyama, a former planning official in the U.S. Department of State, raised a question about the larger meaning of the collapse of communism in Eastern Europe and the Soviet Union. Did the triumph of liberal democracy in the Cold War represent the "end of history"? He was not referring to history as a series of events but to history as a process in which humans struggled to find the best way to govern themselves. One of the first attempts to find meaning in the end of the Cold War, Fukuyama's question generated a tremendous amount of heated yet thoughtful discussion.

In answering the question, Fukuyama pointed to earlier struggles in history when monarchy and then fascism struggled with democracy. Then the Cold War pitted communism against democracy. After the collapse of communism, would everyone agree that the liberal democracy based on concepts of freedom and equality of individuals was the "final form of human government" and therefore the end of history as an evolutionary process? Would the dynamic of events henceforth be concerned only with the implementation policy rather than with basic ideology? Would these ideas also lead to a new way of looking at world maps?

Reading the Map

1. Looking at this map through the prism of ideology leads readers to see two worlds formerly locked in a global struggle: the free world of liberal democracies and its competitor, the communist world, which posed the goal of a stateless society in which the workers would rule.

2. The many new nations on this map represent not only the collapse of the former Soviet empire, but also a different way of looking at the globe: as a world made up of various nation states each pursuing similar goals rather than,

as during the Cold War years, an eternal struggle between the Western nations and the communist countries while a third world looked on.

3. The legend instructs us to focus on just two categories, both defined by political rather than ideological boundaries: the territory of the former Union of Soviet Socialist Republics and its replacement in the post-communist era by the Commonwealth of Independent States.

Working with the Map

To follow the news in the early 1990s, Americans needed to learn the names and locations of the independent states that emerged after the break-up of the USSR. The United Nations quickly recognized the former Soviet republics as independent nations. Excluding Russia itself, fourteen nation states fit this designation. List them according to the following regional groupings:

Baltic states

1.

2.

3.

Nations of the great European lowland

4.

5.

6.

Nations of the Caucasus region

7.

8.

9.

The "Stans" of Central Asia

10.

11.

12.

13.

14.

One-Minute Map Quizzes

Reconstruction, 1865–1877

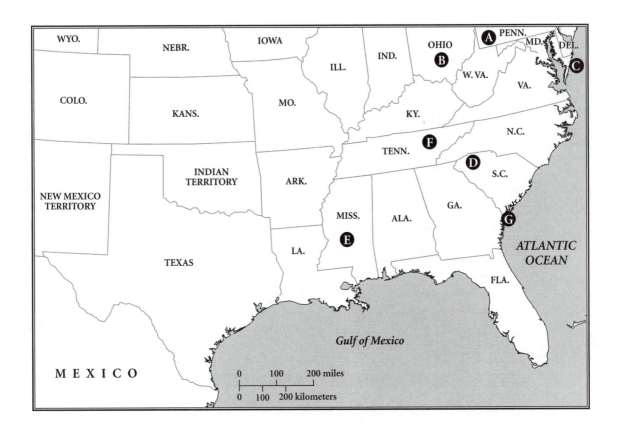

Choose the letter on the map that correctly identifies each of the following:

_____ 1. First former Confederate state readmitted to the Union, 1866

_____ 2. Area of Sea Islands and coastal plantations where General Sherman settled freedmen on 40-acre tracts, 1865

_____ 3. Home state of Radical Republican Thaddeus Stevens

_____ 4. State that sent Hiram R. Revels to the U.S. Senate as its first African American member, 1890

_____ 5. Home state of Republican Party presidential candidate Rutherford B. Hayes, 1876

The Mining Frontier, 1848–1890

Choose the letter on the map that correctly identifies each of the following:

_____ 1. Butte

_____ 2. Deadwood

_____ 3. Cripple Creek

_____ 4. Sutter's Mill

_____ 5. Virginia City

The New South, 1900

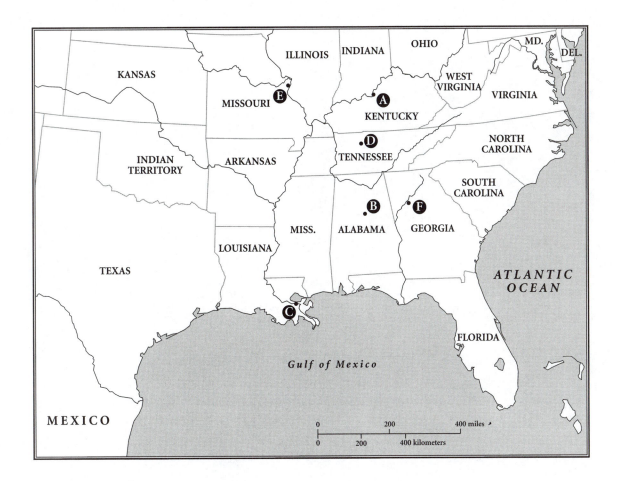

Choose the letter on the map that correctly identifies each of the following cities:

_____ 1. Nashville

_____ 2. Atlanta

_____ 3. New Orleans

_____ 4. Louisville

_____ 5. Birmingham

The Populist Movement in the Late Nineteenth Century

Choose the letter on the map that correctly identifies each of the following sites:

_____ 1. Birthplace of the Southern Alliance

_____ 2. William Jennings Bryan's home state

_____ 3. Site of the "Cross of Gold" speech

_____ 4. Western state that lacked significant Populist support

_____ 5. Home state of fiery Populist orator Mary Elizabeth Lease

America's Cities, 1900

Choose the letter on the map that correctly identifies the following major American cities:

_____ 1. San Francisco

_____ 2. Philadelphia

_____ 3. St. Louis

_____ 4. Chicago

_____ 5. New Orleans

_____ 6. New York

_____ 7. Los Angeles

_____ 8. Minneapolis

_____ 9. Boston

_____ 10. Baltimore

The Woman's Suffrage Movement, 1848–1918

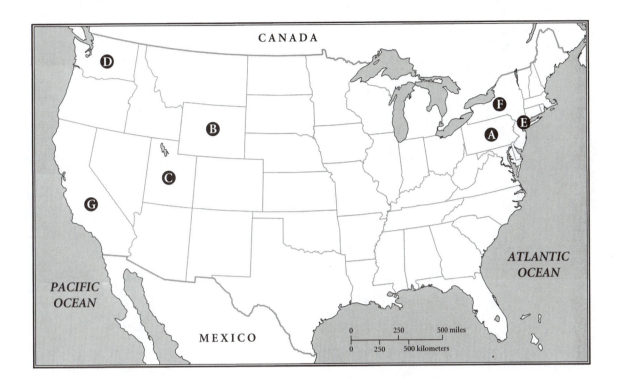

Choose the letter on the map that correctly identifies the location of each of the following places:

_____ 1. Seneca Falls, site of the first women's rights convention, 1848

_____ 2. Wyoming Territory, the first to allow women's suffrage, 1869

_____ 3. A Mormon territory that granted women the right to vote, 1870

_____ 4. The first Pacific state to adopt women's suffrage, 1910

_____ 5. Political organization Tammany Hall which switched sides and supported the movement, 1917

The American Empire in 1917

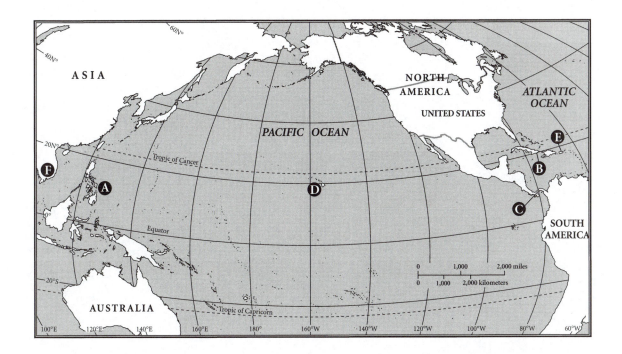

Choose the letter on the map that correctly identifies each of the following locations:

_____ 1. The Philippine Islands

_____ 2. The Hawaiian Islands

_____ 3. Guantanamo naval base

_____ 4. Puerto Rico

_____ 5. Panama Canal Zone

U.S. Participation in World War I, 1917–1918

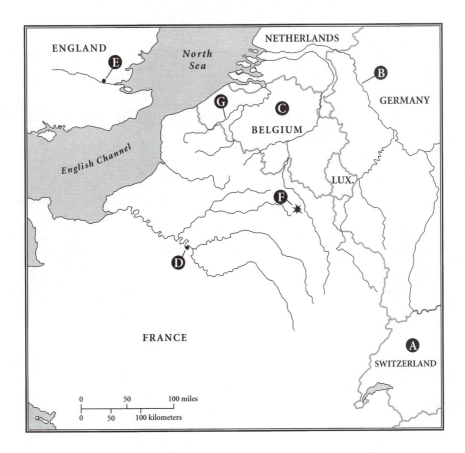

Choose the letter on the map that correctly identifies each of the following locations:

_____ 1. Rhine River

_____ 2. Neutral nation at the source of the Rhine River

_____ 3. London

_____ 4. Paris

_____ 5. Meuse-Argonne

The Shift from Rural to Urban Population, 1920–1930

Choose the letter on the map that correctly identifies each of the following:

_____ 1. Two Gulf coast states that showed strong population growth between 1920 and 1930

_____ 2. A Midwestern city that experienced rapid growth between 1920 and 1930

_____ 3. The portion of Arizona that grew most rapidly between 1920 and 1930

_____ 4. The section of California that grew most dramatically between 1920 and 1930

_____ 5. Western state that saw a significant increase in Ku Klux Klan activity in the 1920s

The Dust Bowl of the 1930s

Choose the letter on the map that correctly identifies the following:

_____ 1. Center of severe drought and wind erosion

_____ 2. Okies route to California

_____ 3. Okies route to Chicago

_____ 4. 100th west meridian

_____ 5. Los Angeles

QUIZ 25

The Tennessee Valley Authority, 1933–1952

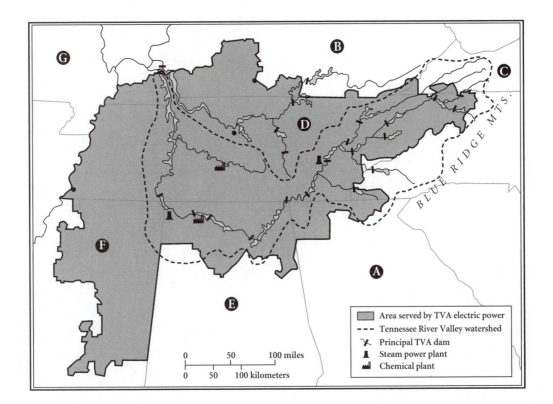

Choose the letter on the map that correctly identifies each of the following states that benefited from the TVA:

_____ 1. Mississippi

_____ 2. Georgia

_____ 3. Virginia

_____ 4. Alabama

_____ 5. Kentucky

World War II in Europe, 1939–1945

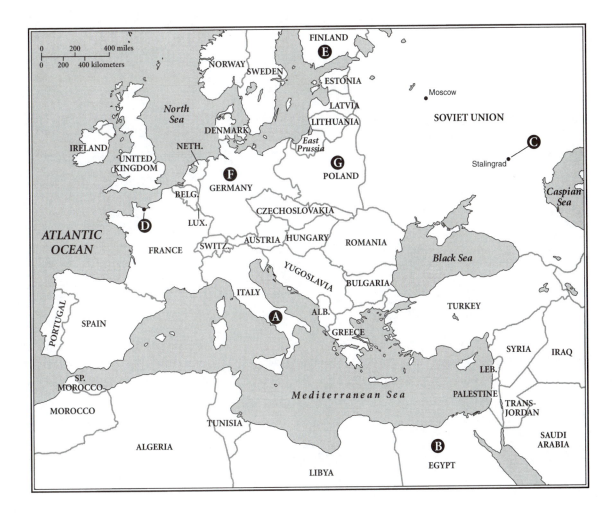

Choose the letter on the map that correctly identifies each of the following:

_____ 1. Nation whose invasion by Germany began the war

_____ 2. The site where the Soviet army launched the massive counterattack that stalled the German army in the winter of 1942 to 1943

_____ 3. Location of Allied offensive against German forces in 1942

_____ 4. Location of Allied offensive against German forces in 1943

_____ 5. Site of the Allied invasion at Normandy on June 6, 1944

The Korean War, 1950–1953

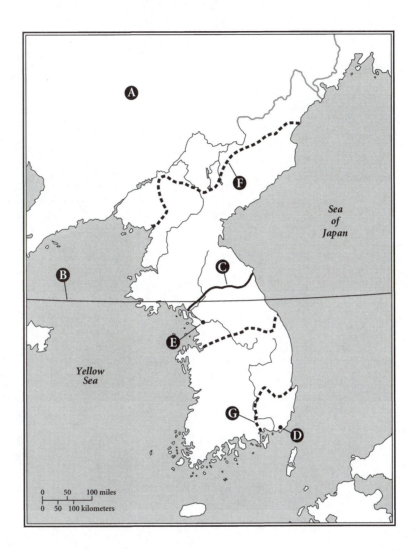

Choose the letter on the map that correctly identifies each of the following:

_____ 1. China

_____ 2. Seoul

_____ 3. Pusan

_____ 4. 38th parallel

_____ 5. Armistice line, July 7, 1953

The Civil Rights Movement, 1954–1965

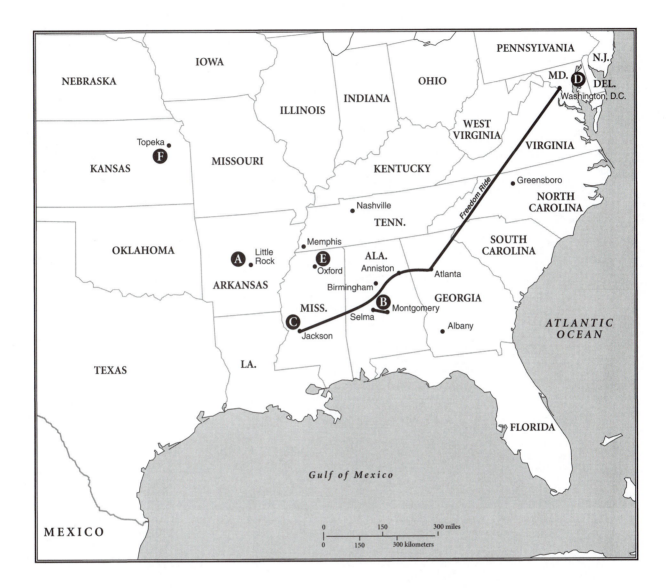

Choose the letter on the map that identifies each of the following cities:

_____ 1. Origin of *Brown v. The Board of Education* lawsuit, 1954

_____ 2. City where Rosa Parks refused to move to the back of the bus, 1955

_____ 3. Where President Eisenhower sent federal troops to enforce integration at Central High School, 1957

_____ 4. City where James Meredith integrated the University of Mississippi under the protection of federal troops, 1962

_____ 5. City where SNCC organized the Freedom Summer voter registration drive, 1964

The Vietnam War, 1964–1975

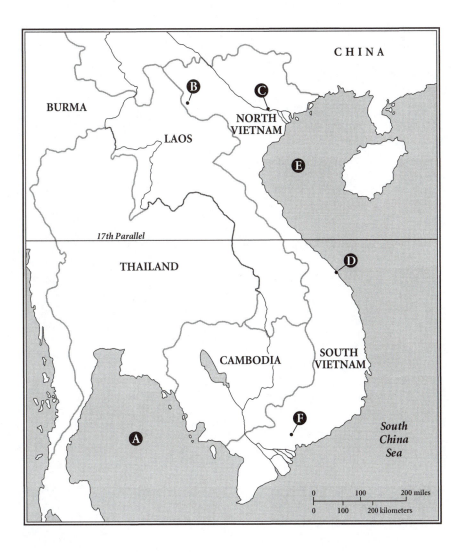

Choose the correct letter on the map that identifies each of the following locations:

_____ 1. Saigon

_____ 2. Dien Bien Phu

_____ 3. Hanoi

_____ 4. Gulf of Tonkin

_____ 5. Gulf of Thailand

United States Involvement in Latin America and the Caribbean, 1954–2000

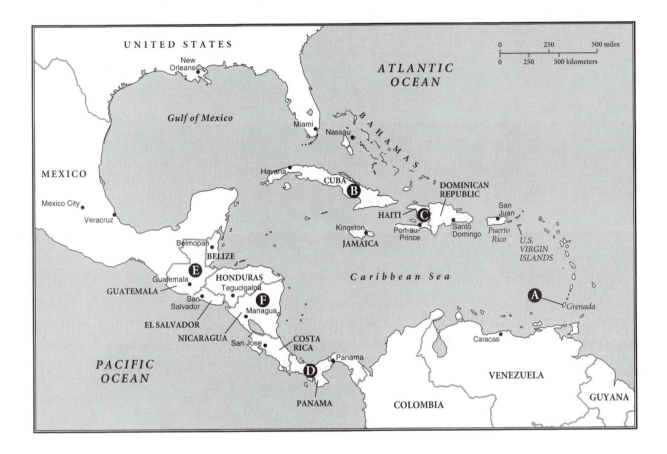

Choose the letter on the map that correctly identifies the location of the following events:

_____ 1. U.S. support for Contra rebels fighting Sandinista government, 1979–1989

_____ 2. U.S. troops invade to oust a communist regime, 1983

_____ 3. CIA-backed Cuban exiles launch unsuccessful invasion at the Bay of Pigs, 1961

_____ 4. U.S. backed coup overthrows Arbenz socialist government, 1954

_____ 5. U.S. troops oversee peaceful return of ousted President Aristide, 1994

United States Involvement in the Middle East, 1980–2002

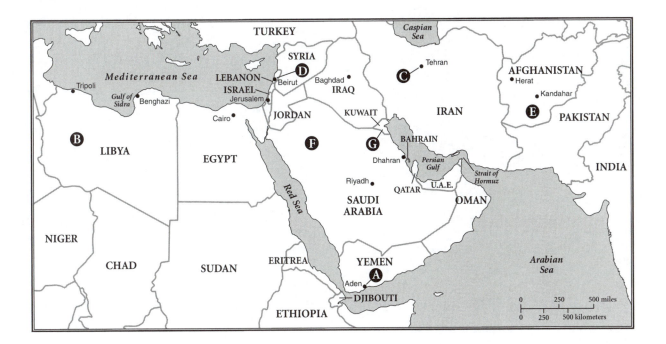

Choose the letter on the map that correctly identifies each of the following events or locations:

_____ 1. Two hundred forty-one U.S. peacekeeping troops killed in terrorist bombing, 1983

_____ 2. U.S.-led war removes the Taliban government from power, 2001–2002

_____ 3. Seventeen U.S. sailors killed in terrorist attack on U.S.S. *Cole*, 2000

_____ 4. U.S. citizens held hostage in American embassy, 1979–1981

_____ 5. Nation invaded by Iraq in 1990 that led to Persian Gulf War

APPENDIXES

Answer Key

Basic Geography

Worksheet C
1-G, 2-E, 3-F, 4-J, 5-H, 6-C, 7-D, 8-I, 9-B, 10-A.

Worksheet D
1-H, 2-D, 3-G, 4-B, 5-E, 6-C, 7-A, 8-I, 9-F, 10-J

Mapping America's History

Worksheet 26
1.E, 2.G, 3.F, 4.I, 5.A, 6.C, 7.B, 8.J, 9.D, 10.H

Worksheet 28
(1) two, (2 & 3) Los Angeles, San Francisco, (4) Rio Grande, (5) Jacksonville, (6) Miami, (7) Michigan, (8) seven, (9) Chicago, (10) Great Lakes, (11) New York, (12) Denver, (13) Oklahoma City, (14) Nashville, (15) Atlanta

Worksheet 29
1.F, 2.H, 3.A, 4.B, 5.C, 6.D, 7.E, 8.G

Worksheet 31
1, 2, 3: Estonia, Latvia, Lithuania; 4, 5, 6: Belarus, Ukraine, Moldova; 7, 8, 9: Georgia, Armenia, Azerbaijan; 10, 11, 12, 13, 14: Kazakhstan, Kyrgyzstan, Uzbekistan, Tajikistan, Turkmenistan

One-Minute Map Quizzes

Quiz 15
1.F, 2.G, 3.A, 4.E, 5.B

Quiz 16
1.B, 2.F, 3.C, 4.D, 5.E

Quiz 17
1.D, 2.F, 3.C, 4.A, 5.B

Quiz 18
1.F, 2.D, 3.A, 4.B, 5.E

Quiz 19
1.G, 2.I, 3.A, 4.J ,5.E, 6.B, 7.H, 8.C, 9.F, 10.D

Quiz 20
1.F, 2.B, 3.C, 4.D, 5.E

Quiz 21
1.A, 2.D, 3.B, 4.E, 5.C

Quiz 22
1.B, 2.A, 3.E, 4.D, 5.F

Quiz 23
1.A, C, 2.E, 3.F, 4.B, 5.G

Quiz 24
1.B, 2.D, 3.E, 4.F, 5.C

Quiz 25
1.F, 2.A, 3.C, 4.E ,5.B

Quiz 26
1.G, 2.C, 3.B, 4.A, 5.D

Quiz 27
1.A, 2.E, 3.D, 4.B, 5.C

Quiz 28
1.F, 2.B, 3.A, 4.E, 5.C

Quiz 29
1.F, 2.B, 3.C, 4.E, 5.A

Quiz 30
1.F, 2.A, 3.B, 4.E, 5.C

Quiz 31
1.D, 2.E, 3.A, 4.C, 5.G

Outline Reference Maps

North America: Physical Geography

0 500 1,000 miles

0 500 1,000 kilometers

The United States: Political Divisions

The World: Physical Geography

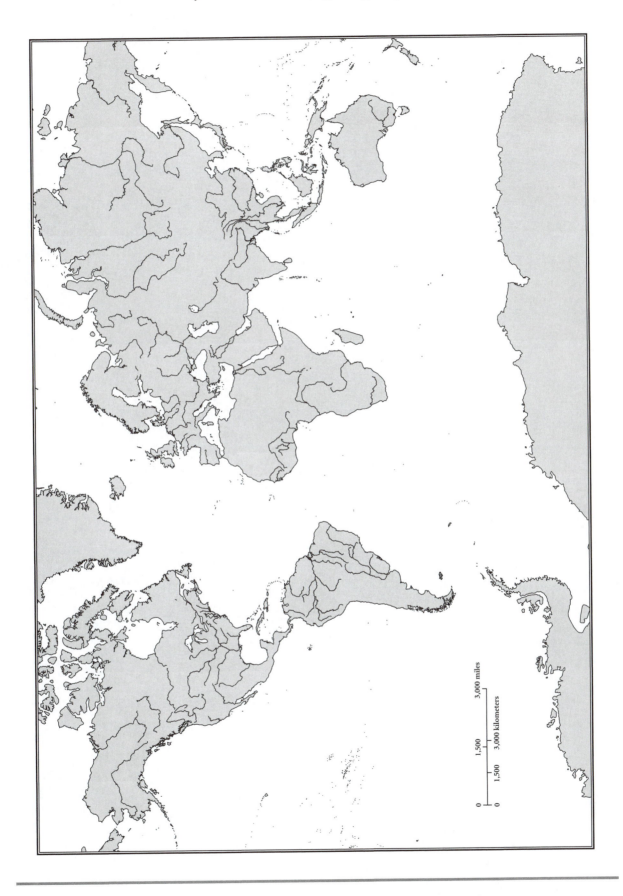

3,000 miles

1,500

3,000 kilometers

1,500

0

0

The World: Political Divisions, 2003

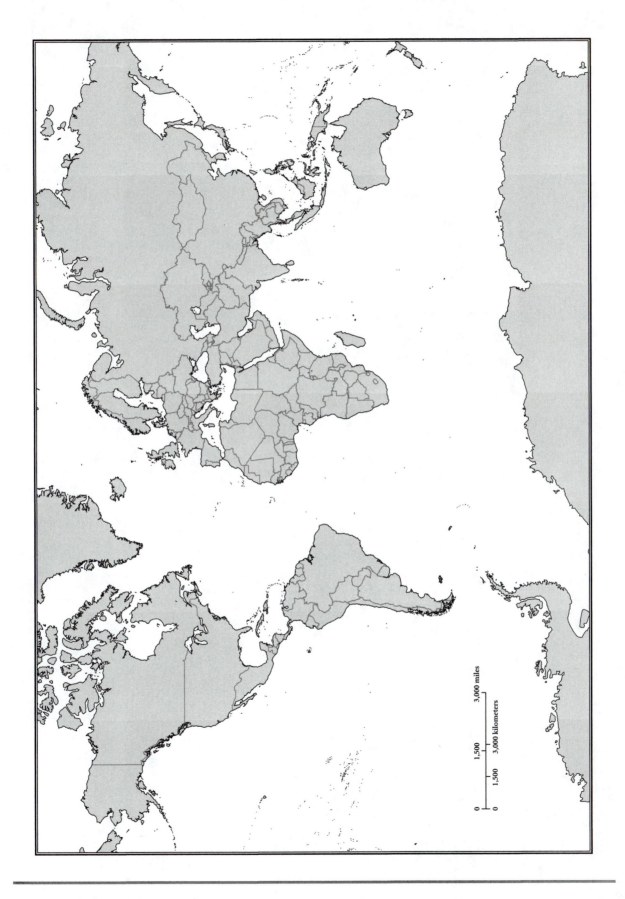

3,000 miles

1,500

0

3,000 kilometers

1,500

0